# MAKING YOUR OWN
# STRINGED
# INSTRUMENTS

## BY DAVID D. CALVERT

**TAB** TAB BOOKS Inc.
BLUE RIDGE SUMMIT, PA. 17214

FIRST EDITION

FIRST PRINTING

Copyright © 1982 by TAB BOOKS Inc.

Printed in the United States of America

Reproduction or publication of the content in any manner, without express permission of the publisher, is prohibited. No liability is assumed with respect to the use of the information herein.

Library of Congress Cataloging in Publication Data

Calvert, David D.
    Making your own stringed instruments.

    Includes index.
    1. Stringed instruments—Construction. I. Title.
ML460.C34   1982       787       82-5910
ISBN 0-8306-2379-5          AACR2
ISBN 0-8306-1379-X (pbk.)

Cover photo courtesy Michael K. Pitzer

# Contents

# Acknowledgments

Thank you:
My many friends who encouraged me in the making of instruments and, especially, the writing of this book.
Ladies who typed chapters and pages of the manuscript.
Mary P. Davis for your assistance in checking the fret spacing for the fingerboard diagrams.
Merle Moore and my friends at the library for your valued help.
Front cover picture: Michael K. Pitzer.
Photography: Larry Lewis and Phil Harris.
Manuscript typing: Brenda Sue Trader and Linda Lou Calvert.
Diagrams: Charles E. Calvert.

This book is dedicated to the memory of Ira McClain, a friend whose advice and encouragement "pushed" me into making musical instruments, and to my family. Each member of my family had something to do with the making of this book.

> *The strings of a lute are alone though they quiver with the same music.*
>
> Kahlil Gibran

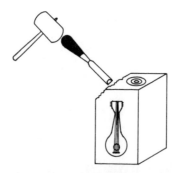

# Preface

Music is as old as mankind. We associate music with happiness. The Garden of Eden must have been a happy place. Genesis 4:21 speaks of those who played the harp and organ. Perhaps Adam sang to Eve, "Let Me Call You Sweetheart."

Even though we associate music with happiness, we sing when we are sad. We also play music and sing when we bury our dead. Music is a form of entertainment. We play the radio while we work, while we study, while we play, and while we eat. Music is played and songs are sung at sports events. I once saw three boys, each about 10 years of age, play ball. Before they began to play, one of the boys sang "The Star Spangled Banner."

Music is more than entertainment. Music is one of our oldest forms of communication. A young man sings love songs to his girlfriend. We sing our children to sleep with lullabies. Armies have been stirred and moved to battle with music. We use music to advertise the products we have for sale.

To possess the ability and talent to play a musical instrument, to sing, to entertain yourself and others surely brings an artist a great amount of pleasure. It greatly enhances that pleasure to make a musical instrument on which you can perform. The purpose of this book is to explain how to make your own musical instrument—an instrument you will be proud to own.

Let me share with you the experience that prompted me to take up the hobby of making instruments. A friend of mine gave my brother a very old mandolin that needed to be repaired. After the

Fig. P-1. A ukulele made in 1945 by a German prisoner of war in an American prison camp.

mandolin was repaired, he was playing it one day when I visited him. I was so thrilled with his mandolin that I said, "I am going home and make a mandolin of my own." A few weeks later—after much trial and error, and frequent trips to the drawing board, so to speak—it was completed. It is not the best looking instrument in the world, but imagine my pleasure and excitement when I was told that it sounded better than many factory-produced instruments.

One Christmas, my son brought me a blank guitar neck. A blank neck is rough (just as it has come from the saw). I started shaping it with the rasp that same day; I intended to make a 12-string guitar. Shortly thereafter, severe, cold winter weather began and lasted for several weeks. There was so much talk of a natural gas shortage to heat our homes that I would not use the gas to heat my shop during that time. Rather than wait until warmer weather, most of the work in making that guitar was done on the kitchen table. It took about two months to complete. One evening, just as I started putting the strings on the guitar, the electricity went off and that guitar was strung by the light of a kerosene lamp. I could not wait for the

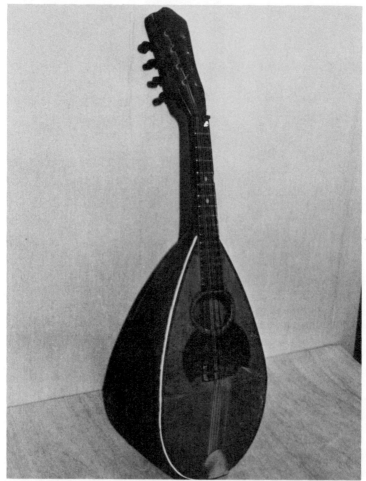

Fig. P-2. A round-back mandolin.

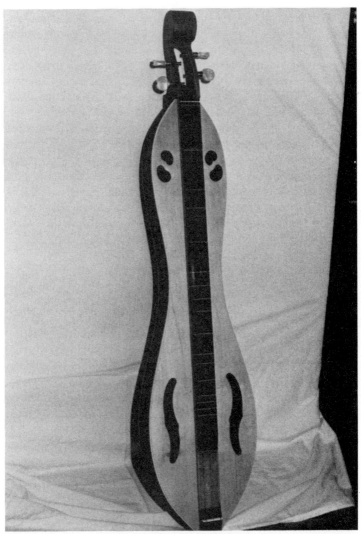

Fig. P-3. A dulcimer that was made in Korea. It was loaned for this photograph by the Best Deal and Colaman store.

electricity to come back on. I am always anxious to string a new instrument to see how it sounds.

Let me assure you that an expensive workshop is not necessary for the projects described in this book. The making of a musical instrument does not require a great amount of space. A garage, a basement, a spare room, or a back yard will do if a workshop is not available.

Man has used his ingenuity in making musical instruments. Crude and simple things such as combs covered with thin paper, saws, washboards, and the like have been used to make music. From the simple instruments to the magnificent organs in majestic cathedrals, we hear the sounds of music. Basically, the instruments of today are the same as they were thousands of years ago. Each country and each culture has its music and musical instruments.

The instrument shown in Fig. P-1 was made in 1945 by a German prisoner of war. He made the ukulele in an American prison of war camp and gave it to an American guard. The body of the instrument was made from the wood of an orange crate. The neck was made from a fence post that had partially rotted away. The instrument was stained with coffee. Frets were made out of metal from a German war plane. The tuning pegs were the violin friction type. It is really a fine piece of work to have been made under a shade tree.

The mandolin in Fig. P-2 is the round-back style. The edge is covered with ivoroid binding. This mandolin has a hollow-like mellow tone.

The dulcimer in Fig. P-3 was loaned to me for this picture by the Best Deal and Colaman Store. This dulcimer was made in Korea. The body is made from a dark wood with a light top. Ivoroid binding was used on this instrument. The tuning pegs are the ukulele type.

Readers are encouraged to see photographs of dulcimers in *The Oxford Junior Companion to Music*, Oxford University Press, 1954. One picture is of a stone dulcimer. It is a huge instrument and the photograph shows it being played by three young men. Perhaps these are the same three young men who played the instrument for Queen Victoria in 1840.

# Chapter 1

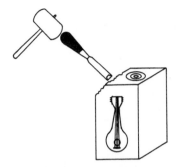

# Introduction

Making musical instruments is a very challenging and satisfying experience. A well-made instrument is a thing of beauty. The tender loving care that all instrument makers have seems to be built into their instruments. Is there anything other than a musical instrument made from inanimate objects, such as wood, glue, and metal, that comes so close to having a personality?

Each person who makes a musical instrument is motivated from within. Perhaps it is the urge to create or the desire to do something not many people do. The urge to make a musical instrument hits people in all walks of life. This includes people who have had experience working with wood and those who can say, "I have never made anything before."

The first mandolin I made is not the best-looking instrument ever made, but I would not part with it. Some people who read this book will not have had any experience working with wood. Others might have worked with wood for many years. I have written this book for the beginner. Experienced woodworkers will find much help in my ideas and instructions.

There are many types of wood that can be used in making instruments. Actually, most woods can be used. A beautiful piece of wood might be suitable for the head or tailpiece of a dulcimer that would not make a good top for an instrument. In the photographs of instruments in this book, you will see different kinds of wood. Mahogany is the only imported wood I used in building the instruments. You will see cherry, maple, walnut, sumac, chestnut, sassafras, and tree of heaven. Some of this wood I cut from trees.

I made the body of my first mandolin from ⅛-inch plywood and I am very pleased with the plywood mandolin. Many people, no doubt, will question the use of plywood in the making of instruments. Nevertheless, there are several valid reasons for building your first instrument from plywood.

Perhaps the most important reason for using plywood to make a mandolin is the quality of the sound and tone it produces. It might seem unbelievable until you listen to its clear, crisp beautiful tone—a tone that improves with age.

Plywood is easy to use. It will not split, crack, or warp as does straight-grained wood. It is difficult to obtain a piece of straight-grained wood that is wide enough to make the front or back of an instrument. Therefore, the pieces must be joined and glued together to make the required width. This is difficult for the inexperienced person to do.

Plywood is easy to obtain and it is relatively inexpensive. It makes a nice looking instrument. Using plywood, the person who is making his first instrument will gain experience in the art. After he has gained experience, he might very well decide to continue the hobby and use other wood in the making of instruments.

It might be possible for you to find suitable scraps or small pieces of plywood at a cabinetmaker's shop. There are detailed instructions in Chapter 10 on making tops and sides of an instrument from straight-grained wood.

My main source of ⅛-inch plywood is regular doors used in building houses. These doors are hollow. Sometimes I can find a damaged door and buy it for much less than a regular door. Often I can find a *cutout*. A cutout is a portion of a door that has been cut out so that a window can be installed in the door.

To prepare a door for use in making instruments, cut away the door framework. Separate the plywood from the cardboard filler. Clean up the glue spots and you have several square feet of excellent plywood to use in making instruments.

The door framework is not waste or scrap; it has many uses around the shop. For example, it can be used to test the depth of the router cut before routing for binding.

Do *not* exert too much pressure on the clamps when clamping wood for gluing. When two pieces of wood are clamped together for gluing, some of the glue is squeezed out. It is possible to press enough out so that the joint will be weakened.

Figure 7-5 shows the use of a guide for a power saw. This guide is used for cutting the soundboard of the hammered dulcimer. This is really an awkward position in which to use the power saw. There is not enough clearance under the saw motor for the guide. Therefore, the guide was used on the other edge of the saw table. Because of this awkward position, the picture shows me holding the board while my son uses the saw.

Work safely! An instrument, regardless of how beautiful it looks or how well it sounds, is not worth losing a hand or a finger. Figure 10-5 shows the guard off the dado heads. The guard was left off only for the picture-taking session. In our shop, we do *not* operate tools without the proper guard in place. We take *all* safety precautions. So Should You!

Work safely and enjoy your work. Build a part of yourself into your instrument and you will have an instrument that will bless your heart.

# Chapter 2

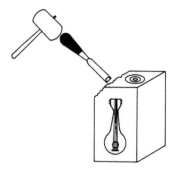

# Material Selection

Sound is caused by vibrations. Vibration occurs when certain objects or things move or crash together. When thing like instrument strings or vocal chords are moved, they vibrate—thus producing sound.

Vibrations are not all alike. They are different in quality, pitch, tone, and clearness. The sound of a high-pitched voice is different from the sound of a low, deep voice. The vibrations caused by the clap of your hands is different from those caused by a streak of lightning. Falling objects create vibrations. Can you hear a pin drop? Yes, but the sound of a falling pin is different from that of a falling tree.

To produce music, a stringed instrument must have a structure over which the strings are strung and tuned to a desired pitch. The instrument must be built strong enough to withstand the stress of the strings. Also, it must be built to maintain the pitch to which the strings are tuned. There must also be something to magnify the vibrations of the strings so that the body of the instrument becomes a sound box. The instrument must be built in such a way as to provide maximum vibrations and sound.

The sound box can be made entirely out of the same kind of wood. For example, a sound box made from ⅛-inch plywood will produce sharp, clear tones. To get maximum vibration out of this instrument, the back of the sound box must be glued to the inside cross bracing. The front is not glued to the bracing; it is allowed to float, so to speak. This allows for freedom of vibration.

Another method of building the sound box is to use a straight-grained wood to make the top. A soft wood seems to have an absorbing effect that gives a softer, more mellow tone to the instrument.

From one instrument, you hear a sharp, crisp tone and from another instrument you hear a soft, mellow tone. Which is the best sound? It is really a matter of preference. Some people prefer one sound and some the other.

Look for eye appeal in an instrument. Nature has given us some beautiful woods. You can add variety to an instrument by the wise use of different wood in its construction. You can make a beautiful

Fig. 2-1. A mandolin.

Fig. 2-2. A mandolin with a sumac top.

instrument while maintaining a handmade look. Too much pearl inlay seems to make a handmade instrument look like it came out of the store. The wise use of a combination of wood enhances the beauty of an instrument, and in certain cases the sound might be improved.

Figure 2-1 shows my first mandolin. It has a plywood body, a maple neck, and a store-bought fingerboard.

Figure 2-2 shows the mandolin that is my pride and joy. The back and sides are plywood-stained Spanish oak. It has a maple neck and a walnut fingerboard. The top was made from sumac. Sumac is really a bush. It has few uses because the wood is pithy. The wood I used was 3½ inches in diameter. Because it is a pithy, grained wood, I glued it to a veneer backing before sanding. Sumac is a beautiful wood. Its colors are white, brown, green, and yellow.

The mandolin shown in Fig. 2-3 is made from Philippine mahogany (except the neck). This is a beautiful instrument. It has a soft, mellow tone. The neck and bridge were made from walnut. The

Fig. 2-3. A mandolin with an all-mahogany body.

Fig. 2-4. The sides of this mandolin are painted red, white, and blue.

nut on this mandolin is Corian. Corian is a synthetic material that can be used like wood; however, it is difficult to find.

Figure 2-4 shows a mandolin. The sides are painted red, white, and blue. Figure 2-5 shows a mandolin case. This mandolin has a mahogany top. The neck is walnut and the fingerboard was made from sassafras wood. A strip of walnut was inlaid between the fourth and fifth frets.

The dulcimer shown in Fig. 2-6 is the first dulcimer I made. The owner of an abandoned strip mine operation gave me permission to cut a piece of wood off a wild cherry tree that had been left lying there to rot. I cut the log and hauled it out in the trunk of my car

Fig. 2-5. A mandolin case.

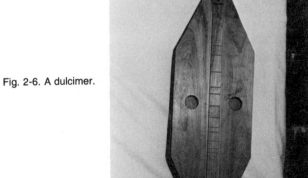

Fig. 2-6. A dulcimer.

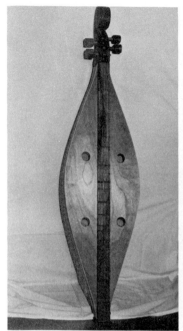

Fig. 2-7. A dulcimer.

Fig. 2-8. A guitar.

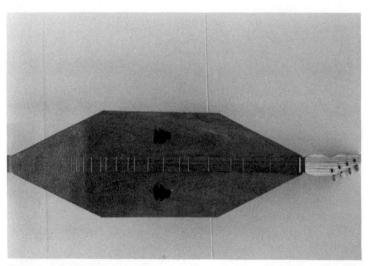

Fig. 2-9. A dulcimer.

10

Fig. 2-10. A ukulele.

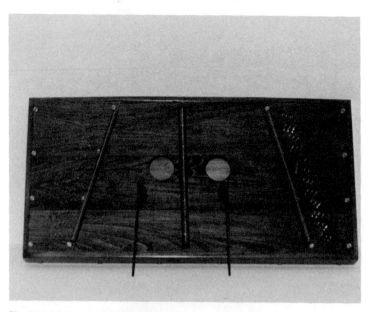

Fig. 2-11. A hammered dulcimer.

Fig. 2-12. A guitar.

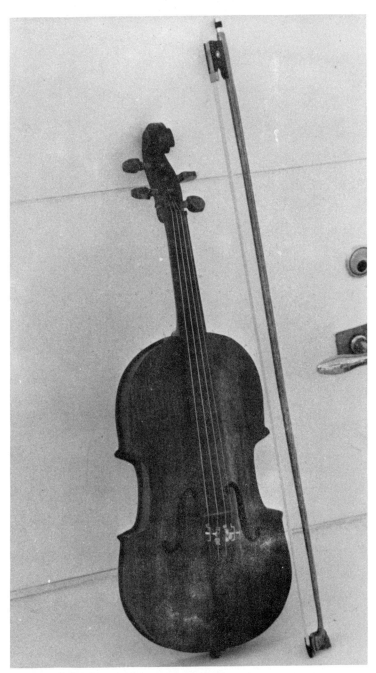

Fig. 2-13. A violin.

Fig. 2-14. The back of a violin.

to the sawmill where it was sawed into lumber. The dulcimer shown in the photograph was made from that wood.

Figure 2-7 shows another shaped dulcimer I made for a friend. It was made from plywood.

Figure 2-8 shows a guitar I made. The preceding photographs are of instruments detailed in this book. Figure 2-9 shows a ukelele. Figure 2-10 shows a plucked dulcimer. Figure 2-11 shows a hammered dulcimer. Figure 2-12 shows a guitar. Figure 2-13 shows a violin. Figure 2-14 shows the back of a violin.

# Chapter 3

# Mandolin

When I started making my 12-string guitar, I first bought the nut. It was necessary for me to start with the nut because I was going to make the fingerboard and I needed to have the nut so I would know how wide to make the fingerboard and the neck of the guitar. The starting point for making your own mandolin should be the fingerboard. You must decide if you want to make the fingerboard or buy it. I recommend that you buy the fingerboard for your first instrument. If you do buy it, be sure it is already fretted. If you do make the fingerboard, make it according to the dimensions given in Fig. 3-1.

### THE NECK

The wood used for the neck must be a hard, close-grained wood. Hard maple makes an excellent neck. Curly maple, if you can find it, will make a better looking neck than just ordinary hard maple. You can use walnut, mahogany, or some other suitable wood. A 15-inch length of 2-×-4 lumber will be sufficient size for the neck.

If a piece of wood 2 inches thick is not available, it is possible to use a thinner piece. Glue it together to get the proper thickness for the head and heel of the neck. The thinner piece of wood can be as small as 1 inch thick and 2¾ inches wide. It must be at least 23 inches long. If the wood for the neck is not already smooth and even enough to glue the fingerboard to it, first run the neck over a jointer to make it smooth and even. Figures 3-2 and 3-3 show how to mark the neck so that it can be cut out properly. If the piece of wood is only 1 inch thick, two pieces must be cut off the board to form the heel and head of the neck. See Fig. 3-4 for a view of gluing process.

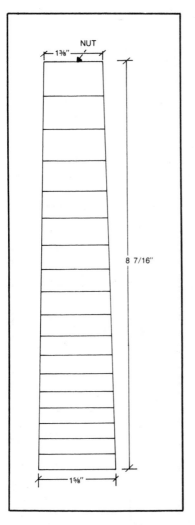

Fig. 3-1. The pattern for a mandolin fingerboard.

The piece of wood that is to be glued to the underside of the neck to form the heel should be 3 inches long. Before cutting it off the main board, cut an angle on the end that will form the angle of the heel. See arrows 6 and 7 in Fig. 3-3. The angle is cut at 45 degrees or sloped back 1 inch. The block of wood that forms the heel is to be glued on (arrow 6 in Fig. 3-3) and extends to the heel end of the neck.

Cut a piece of wood (5 inches in length) off the same board and glue it to the underside of the neck wood. This piece of wood is glued on (at arrow 5 in Fig. 3-3) and extends to the end of head. The

17

glue joints should be as neat as possible. They will show, but they should be as inconspicuous as you can make them.

After the glue has had sufficient time to dry, make a center mark the complete length of the neck wood. This mark will be on the top of the neck. The center mark (from arrow 3 in Fig. 3-2 to the heel end of the neck) will be an important reference line all the time you are making your instrument. If it begins to wear away, it should be remarked.

Mark the neck as shown in Fig. 3-2. Be sure the saw cuts are made outside the marks so that there will be wood left all around the edges to sand away the saw marks. Then mark and cut the neck as in Fig. 3-5.

The neck should be cut out with a band saw. If you do not have a band saw, try to get someone at a vocational school or a cabinet-

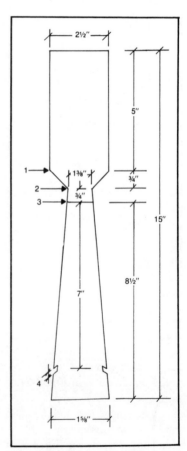

Fig. 3-2. The front view of a mandolin neck.

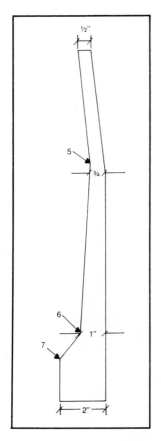

Fig. 3-3. The side view of a mandolin neck.

maker to cut the neck out for you. Caution the band saw operator not to cut too deep at arrows 2, 5, and 6, as shown in Figs. 3-2 and 3-3. It is better to leave extra wood at these places to be worked away with the rasp than to leave a saw cut so deep that it cannot be worked out. Such saw cuts, and I have had them, will ruin a neck or show up as poor workmanship throughout the life of the instrument.

A neck can also be cut out on a table saw, but it is more difficult. If you cut the neck out on a table saw be extremely careful at arrows 2 and 5 as shown in Figs. 3-2 and 3-3. Stop the saw before you get to the crucial points and finish the cuts with a hand saw. Take your time in measuring and cutting out the neck. Proportion it well. Your mandolin neck will be a thing of beauty and a masterpiece of workmanship.

After the neck has been cut out, begin shaping it with the wood rasp (Fig. 3-6). You can clamp the neck to a workbench or clamp a

V-shaped piece of wood to the bench to hold the neck while using the rasp. Cover one end of the rasp with a heavy cloth or use gloves to protect your hand from becoming sore and tender from using the rasp. Work on the backside of the neck until it is round or a half-moon shape. The neck should also be tapered. It should be about ¾ inch thick, at arrow 2 of Fig. 3-2, and tapered all the way back until it is about 1 inch thick at the heel. The main thing is to work at it until you are satisfied with it and until it suits you.

## THE SIDES

The body of the instrument is made from ⅛-inch plywood. The sides are made from a strip of plywood bent into a band according to the shape you choose for the mandolin. The exact shape or size is not so important. A variation of ½ inch, more or less, in the size or shape will have only a slight effect on its appearance and the sound it produces.

Fig. 3-4. Gluing a heel to a mandolin neck.

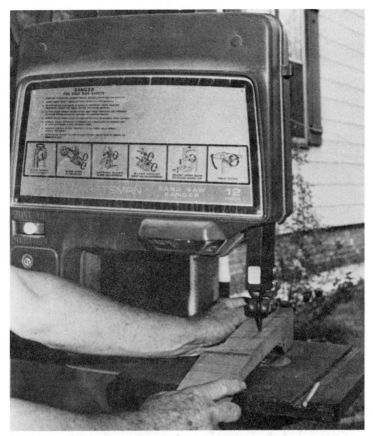

Fig. 3-5. Cutting out the mandolin neck on a band saw.

## Making the Form

A form (Fig. 3-7) of some kind is necessary to band the sides around. You might already have an object around your shop or house that will make a suitable form you can use to bend the band. A form can be made from ½-inch plywood or any other suitable wood. Cut it to shape and nail two pieces together to get proper thickness. Strips of wood about ½ inch thick can be used between the two plies to get the proper thickness. These strips leave the center open and allow air to pass. This aids the sides in drying.

Blocks of wood should be cut to fit the outside of the form (as in Fig. 3-8). The form actually becomes a clamp in itself when the gluing clamps are tightened. This form is used to bend the sides to shape and to glue two side pieces together. The center of the form must be marked so that the sides can be positioned properly on the form for bending.

## Cutting the Sides

After the form has been made, cut a piece of ⅛-inch plywood 31½ inches long (or the same length as the measurement around the form). The width of the sides will be determined by the thickness of the neck (at arrow 4, Fig. 3-2). The front of the instrument will be recessed ⅛ inch into the neck. If the neck is 2 inches thick (at arrow 4, Fig. 3-2), the sides should be cut 1⅞ inches wide. Mark the center of the side piece so that it is the same length on each side of the mark. This mark should be on inside of the side piece.

Fig. 3-6. Shaping the mandolin neck.

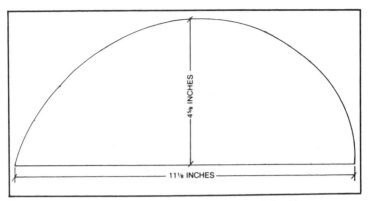

Fig. 3-7. A diagram of one side of a form to bend mandolin sides.

## Bending the Sides

Place the sides in the bathtub or any suitable container. Cover it with water and soak it for at least an hour or until pliable. After the sides have been soaked and it is pliable, match the mark on the inside of the sides with the center mark on the form.

Bend the sides around the form, place blocks in position, and clamp until the wood has had time to dry at least 24 hours. Figure 3-9 shows the vat I use for soaking wood.

## Cutting Slots in the Neck for the Sides

When the side piece has dried, remove it from the form. Slots must be cut in the neck for the sides to be glued into (see arrow 4,

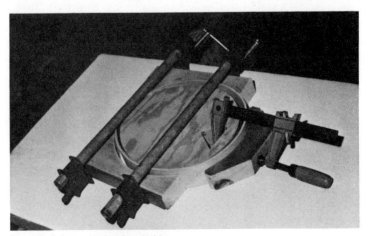

Fig. 3-8. A form used to bend sides.

Fig. 3-9. A vat used for soaking wood.

Fig. 3-2). The slots are to be cut in each side of the neck at the heel 7 inches from arrow 3 shown in Fig. 3-2. These slots are to be cut square with the neck, but at a slant into the neck to match the slope of the ends of the sides. A piece of wood clamped to the neck, even with the pencil mark, helps to get the saw started without gouging up the side of the wood that will be outside the instrument.

After this cut has been made at least ¼ inch deep, move the guide piece of wood (that has been clamped to the neck) toward the end of the neck ⅛ or ¼ inch. Depending on how you intend to line the band, make another saw cut here the same depth and angled the same way as the first cut. Working in the last saw cut, splinter the wood between the two cuts with a knife. Be careful not to damage the wood at the first saw cut because this will be outside the instrument and show as poor workmanship. See Fig. 3-10. These slots can also be cut with a band saw.

### Recessing the Top into the Neck

The top of the mandolin must be recessed into the neck ⅛ inch deep. Make a saw cut on the face of the neck in line with the saw cuts made for the slots for the sides. With a rasp or knife, work off the wood from this saw cut back to the end of the neck. At the lower end of the neck, work away about ¼ inch of wood and taper it back to ⅛ inch at the saw cut. If this is not done now, it will need to be done before the top can be glued to the sides. If the neck is not already cut off square and even, now is the time to square it up. The top must be even with the face of the neck so that the fingerboard will fit evenly on the neck and top.

## Assembly of Neck and Sides

The assembly of neck and sides is one of the most crucial steps in the making of a mandolin. The neck and body must be tilted slightly in relation to each other. See Fig. 3-11. The purpose of this tilt is to have enough space between the top of the mandolin and the strings for the bridge.

## Measuring Tilt between Neck and Sides

The bridge should be about ⅜ inch thick and the saddle should be ¼ inch above the bridge. This will make a total bridge height of not more than ⅝ inch. See the section in this chapter on making the bridge. A higher bridge does not look as good as a bridge of this height.

Because you do not have the fingerboard glued on the neck or the bridge made, you must allow for these. At arrow 3 in Fig. 3-2, make a pencil mark across the neck. This is where the narrow end of the fingerboard will be located. At 13½ inches from this mark is where the bridge will be placed. At this point is where you measure to get the proper tilt between neck and body. See Fig. 3-11.

Fit the ends of the side piece into the slots you have already cut in the neck. When they fit snugly in the slots, you have very little tilt between the neck and sides. Actually they should be in perfect alignment—which you do not want. You want to tilt the sides down in relation to the neck.

Fig. 3-10. Cutting slots in the neck for sides.

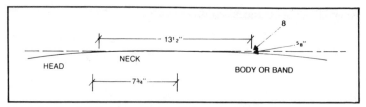

Fig. 3-11. The "tilt" between the mandolin neck and sides.

On the lower side of each end of the side piece, make a mark 1/16 inch back from the end. Draw a line from this mark to the end of the upper side of the wood. Work off the wood back to the mark on each end of the sides with the rasp. Fit the sides in the slots in the neck and then measure the tilt at the predetermined point. Follow this procedure until you have achieved the required tilt between the sides and the neck. When you are satisfied that the ends of the sides are cut at the proper angle, you are ready to glue the neck and sides together.

## Gluing the Neck and Sides

Figure 3-12 shows the neck and sides being glued together. I have a line drawn along the center of my gluing board. A hole is cut in the board to allow the C-clamp to be hooked under the board to clamp the neck in place. The neck is marked on the center at each end. These marks are aligned with the center line on the board. The exact center of the side piece is marked and this mark is positioned on the center line.

In Fig. 3-12, you can see the strip of plywood between the end of the neck and the gluing board. This strip spaces the sides properly at the recessed end of the neck. Another strip of wood, ⅜ inch thick, can be seen between the sides and the gluing board. This strip is located at the bridge position on the mandolin and holds the sides at the proper tilt. Waxed paper must be used at the glue joints to keep the unit from becoming glued to the board.

Hold the pieces together with a block of wood and a C-clamp. Use a good glue and allow 24 hours drying time.

The tension of the strings will have a tendency to pull the sides out of the slots in the neck. To prevent this, make a wedge-shaped block of wood to fit perfectly on each side of the neck and sides. These blocks should be about as long as the part of the neck that is inside the mandolin. Glue them in place and this will give all the support needed to hold the sides in the neck slots. Figure 3-13 shows these wedges in place.

Fig. 3-12. Gluing the neck and sides.

## LINING, BRACING, AND THE END BLOCK

**Lining.** The sides must be lined inside to provide enough surface to glue the front and the back. There are two methods for doing this. The easiest and fastest way to line the sides is to make two side pieces the same width and length and glue them together. A double band is rigid and easy to work with.

Both pieces must be soaked and bent around the form (Fig. 3-7). Also, they should be fastened to the form while the glue dries. The two side pieces must be glued together before they are fitted to the neck for the tilt between the neck and body of the mandolin.

Another method of lining the sides is accomplished by gluing strips of ⅛-inch plywood, ½ inch wide, along the inside edges of the sides. These strips must be held with the C-clamp until the glue dries. When you use this method of lining, the sides are glued to the neck before the lining.

Fig. 3-13. Inside bracing.

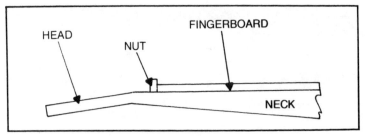

Fig. 3-14. The mandolin head, neck, fingerboard, and nut.

**Bracing.** The instrument must be braced inside, between the front and back. If it is not braced inside, the tension of the strings will push the front of the mandolin downward.

The bracing must be made out of rigid wood. I find that ½-inch plywood makes good bracing. Cut in ½ × ¾ of an inch and follow Fig. 3-14 to assemble. Or for the bracing you can use a ¾ inch corner moulding purchased at a lumberyard. The bracing should be located under the bridge. The bracing must be glued to the sides and back of the mandolin.

**End Block.** Using a straightedge, make a mark on the inside of the sides that lines up with the center line on the neck. Select a piece of wood 2½ inches wide and at least ½ inch thick. Cut it the same length that your sides are wide. Using a rasp, round it off on one side until it fits inside the side piece. Be sure that it is centered on the mark you have made. Glue it to the inside of the sides with wood glue. The purpose of the end block is to have somewhere to fasten the tailpiece.

Allow enough drying time for these glue joints, then—with a rasp and sandpaper—work down both edges of the sides until the band will lay flat on a smooth surface. If there are high spots, work them down until both sides are even all the way around. Refer to Fig. 3-13 when making the wedges, bracing, and end blocks.

## THE BACK AND THE TOP

**Cutting Out the Back.** Place the sides and neck on a piece of ⅛-inch plywood to mark out for cutting. There is an angle of wood on the bottom edge of the heel that you must rasp away to allow the sides to lay flat. This angle is caused when you tilt the neck and the sides. Mark the plywood with pencil on the outside of the sides. The back can be cut out using a sabre saw, a keyhole saw, a band saw, or whatever you have. Do not attempt to cut right on the line; allow extra wood to be worked away with the rasp or router. You are now ready to glue the back on and your instrument is beginning to take shape.

Do not attempt to use C-clamps to glue the back and top to the sides. Instead, place the back on a sturdy table or a smooth floor. Lay the sides down on the back wood. Using a piece of ½-inch plywood or any suitable material on the top side of the band, weight it down with bricks or heavy objects and allow the glue to set. Glue the back to the bracing. Be sure that the weight is evenly distributed. Rubber bands can also be used to hold the back and top while the glue dries. See Fig. 3-15.

*Caution.* When rubber bands are used to hold a back or top while gluing, the top and back must be cut to fit. The rubber bands will pull down on the excess top or back wood and twist the wood. Straight-grained wood will be split if you use rubber bands unless it is cut to the exact shape and size of the sides.

**The Top.** Cut out the top of the mandolin the same way you cut out the back. Now you are ready to cut out the sound hole. Hold the top in place on the unfinished instrument and make a pencil mark on the top to line up with the mark on the center of the neck. Continue to hold the top in place while holding the straightedge along the center line on the neck. Mark the center of the top close to the tail end of the mandolin. Mark the sides and top in relation to each other so when you glue the top on it will be in the same position as when the sound hole position was marked.

Measure 11 inches from arrow 3 in Fig. 3-2. Mark the top at this point. Next use a straightedge along the neck center line and, at the mark on the top, you should now be able to make an X. This is the center of the sound hole position.

Fig. 3-15. Rubber bands are used to hold the top in place while it is being glued.

## CUTTING THE SOUND HOLE

The neatest way to cut the sound hole is by using a hole saw. See Fig. 3-16. A hole saw is an attachment for an electric drill. Drill a starter hole for the bit of the hole and saw at the midway mark you made. Use the 2-inch blade from the assortment of sizes of hole-saw blades. First cut a 2-inch hole out of a piece of ⅛-inch plywood and use this as a bumper between the base of the saw attachment and the top of your mandolin. It will keep the base of the saw from marring the surface of the top. Proceed to cut out the 2-inch sound hole.

If you do not have a hole saw, the sound hole can be cut by hand tools. Use a compass and mark a 2-inch circle at the midway point. Then drill a hole in the center of the circle and, using a keyhole saw or sabre saw, proceed to cut out the sound hole by hand. You will need to use the rasp and sandpaper to smooth the inside of the sound hole after cutting it out. Follow the same procedure to glue the top to the mandolin body as you used in gluing the back. Again, let me caution you not to use clamps; distribute the weight evenly.

## TRIMMING THE EDGES

Refer to Chapter 11 on binding. The edges of the mandolin must either be routed for binding or trimmed before the fingerboard can be glued to the neck. The same method used for routing for binding is used for trimming the edges. It is a matter of setting the depth of cut of the router bit.

The edges can be trimmed by hand. A rasp and sandpaper is all that is required.

## THE FINGERBOARD

If you decide to make the fingerboard for your mandolin, you will need a fret saw to cut the slots for the frets. This saw, along with fret wire and binding, can be ordered by mail (see suppliers).

Cut the fingerboard 8½ inches long and 1⅝ inches wide. Follow the instructions given in this chapter and cut the slots for the frets before tapering the fingerboard to the size as given in Fig. 3-1.

When I started making instruments, I used black stain on the fingerboard. Frankly, I cannot stain a fingerboard so that it will please me. Therefore, I make my fingerboards plain. I glue them on after staining the instrument and finish the fingerboard along with the instrument. I do not attempt to make an instrument look exactly like it was factory made (a handmade instrument should look different than one that comes off the assembly line).

The fingerboard should be made of a hard, close-grained wood like the neck. It should be no more than ¼ inch thick after dressing down to the proper smoothness. Be sure the ends are cut square.

## Cutting Fret Slots

Mark the spacing for the frets exactly as shown in Fig. 3-1. If the distance between the frets is not correct, your mandolin will not sound right. Proper fret spacing is essential in order to get the exact pitch of a note. Use a wooden miter box to cut the fret slots. Cut a

Fig. 3-16. Cutting a sound hole with a drill press.

Fig. 3-17. Cutting saw kerfs in a fingerboard.

new slot for the fret saw in the miter box; those already made are too large for the fret saw. See Fig. 3-17. Make sure the slots are cut deep enough for the fret, but not so deep as to ruin the fingerboard. When you have finished sawing the fret slots, taper the fingerboard to the size shown in Fig. 3-1.

Draw a center line on the back, of the fingerboard. Measure from the line to each edge of the fingerboard to taper. It should be 1⅜ × 1⅝ inches. Cut and taper each side of the board. If the tapered portion is cut off one side only, the frets will not be square across the neck.

## Pin the Fingerboard to the Neck

On the back of the fingerboard, mark the center between frets 2 and 3, and 7 and 8. On the center line, drill a small-diameter hole half way through the fingerboard. Drill holes to match these in the neck.

Be sure the end of the fingerboard is properly spaced at arrow 3. The holes in the neck should be ¼ inch deep. Pins to fit these holes can be made from nails or wire. Use the pins to hold the fingerboard to the neck while you are sanding. Sanding should be completed before the frets are hammered in.

Take a flat piece of metal thin enough to pass through the slots you have cut in the fingerboard. Use this metal to clean the saw dust out of the slots before you drive in the frets.

## INSTALLING FRETS

Place the fingerboard on a solid surface such as a table or work bench. Hold the fret wire in one hand and start tapping it in the slot

Fig. 3-18. Installing frets.

33

with light taps of the hammer. Be sure that the hammer head is smooth; a hammer with a rough head will mar the frets. Tap the fret lightly all the way across until it is partially seated. Cut the end off with a wire cutter. With a flat metal object such as a flat-sided chisel placed on the fret, hammer the fret all the way in the slot. See Fig. 3-18.

## FILING FRET ENDS

Figures 3-19 and 3-20 show the filing of frets. After all the frets have been set in the board, file off the ends even with the edge of the fingerboard. File each fret until the end of the fret has been filed at an angle toward the center of the fingerboard. File both ends of the frets the same way; they should slope toward the center of the fingerboard. Then file the fret ends even with the edge of the fingerboard. When you have the frets filed to your satisfaction, use fine sandpaper to remove any sharp edges from the fret ends. Crocus cloth also can be used on the fret ends.

## FINGERBOARD INLAYS

Inlays in the fingerboard are optional. Pearl inlays can be bought and used for the fingerboard. If you intend to use inlays, they must be inlaid before the fingerboard is glued to the neck. You could choose to use one inlay centered perfectly between the fourth and fifth frets. Follow this procedure to inlay the pearl. First have the inlay on hand. Select a wood bit the same diameter as the inlay. With a drill press, drill a hole in a scrap piece of wood that is the exact thickness as the fingerboard. Set the drill press to drill only as deep as the inlay. After you have set the drill press, you are ready to drill the hole in the fingerboard for the inlay. Pearl inlays can be glued in with contact cement. See Fig. 3-21.

## GLUING THE FINGERBOARD TO THE NECK

Figure 3-22 shows how to glue the fingerboard to the neck. A thick piece of wood is used between frets and clamps so that pressure will be even. This protects the back of the neck from being damaged by the clamps.

## LEVELING THE FRETS

After the fingerboard has been glued to the neck, place a straightedge across the frets (lengthwise along the fingerboard). The straightedge should rest on all the frets. If there are some frets

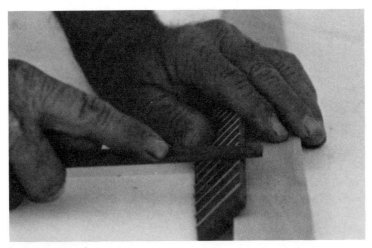

Fig. 3-19. Filing fret ends.

higher than the rest, take a flat file and file these high frets down until they are all level and even.

## KEYS AND TAILPIECE

The best way to drill the holes in the head of the mandolin for the keys is to use a template. The template should be made from wood at least ¾ inch thick. The thicker the template the better job you can do drilling the holes for the keys if you use a hand drill. Drill

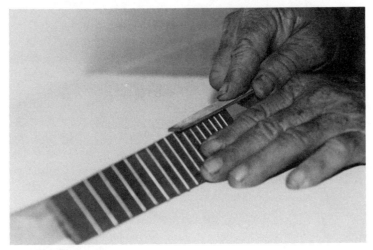

Fig. 3-20. Filing frets.

Fig. 3-21. Drilling the fingerboard for inlays.

the holes for the keys with a drill press, if at all possible. See Fig. 3-23. The template should be cut in the same shape and the same size as the head. Examine the keys closely before drilling the holes in the template. There is a right and left key. See Fig. 3-24. The keys should be installed so that the key mechanism is lower on the instrument than the turning peg part of the key. In other words, it should be lower toward the body of the instrument.

The edge of the keyplate should be set in from the edge of the mandolin head about ⅛ of an inch. Mark the holes properly on the template and drill them with a ¼-inch wood bit. Drill from the front

Fig. 3-22. Gluing the fingerboard to the neck.

rather than from the back if at all possible. Drilling from the back side of the head might splinter the head on the front when the bit comes through the wood. If the keys fit too tightly in the holes after they have been drilled, you might need to ream the holes with a 9/32 steel bit.

## Attaching the Keys to the Head

When you are ready for this operation, insert the keys into position and mark the screw holes. With a small-diameter bit, drill a starter hole about ¼ inch deep (do not drill all the way through). I have never bought a set of keys that contained the screws to install the keys to the head. You will need to buy the screws from a hardware store.

Fig. 3-23. Drilling for keys on a drill press.

Fig. 3-24. The back of mandolin keys.

After the starter holes have been drilled, rub a screw on a bar of soap or paraffin and work it into the wood the proper distance. Remove and follow the same procedure until all the holes have been reamed out. It will be necessary to cut off the tip end of the screws if they are too long.

### Fitting the Tailpiece

The instrument is nearly completed and you are anxious to hear what it will sound like. At this point, if the nut and bridge have not been made, then you must do that before installing the tailpiece.

To find the proper position for the tailpiece, you must use either two pieces of fine wire or two of the mandolin strings, use fine wire if possible. Make a small loop in one end of each wire and attach each loop to the outside hooks on the tailpiece. Fasten the other ends of wire to the first key hole on each side that is next to the fingerboard. Tighten until snug. Be sure the wires are in the outside notches of the nut.

While you hold the tailpiece by hand, move the tailpiece back and forth until the wires line up with the edges of the fingerboard. When the tailpiece position has been found, mark the screw hole with pencil, remove the tailpiece, and drill starter holes. Fasten the tailpiece securely with screws. With the small wires still in place, adjust the nut and bridge for height as much as possible according to the instructions in the following section of this chapter.

## MAKING THE NUT AND BRIDGE

**The Nut.** The nut on a musical instrument is located at the narrow end of the fingerboard. It is slotted for the strings and, along with the bridge saddle, holds and carries the strings over the fingerboard from the keys to the tailpiece.

I have never been able to buy a nut with the string slots already cut. The nuts sold at the music store are blank and the string slots must be cut in them. It is difficult to cut the slots in the blank nuts I buy. When I try to cut the slots for the strings, the edges break off. So instead I use hard wood, plastic, or Corian for the nut. Corian is a synthetic substance that can be worked like wood. The nut on the mandolin shown in Fig. 2-3 was made from Corian. This material is soft enough to work with and hard enough to withstand the pressure of the strings. Also, I have a plastic material that makes an excellent nut for an instrument. It is not plexiglass. The plastic does not break, crack, or splinter. It is see-through clear and it is easy to work with.

The nut should be ¼ of an inch thick and as high as necessary to clear the frets by at least 3/32 of an inch. The top of the nut should slope slightly in the same direction as the slope of the head. To hold the nut in place, drill a small hole about ¼ inch deep in the center of the neck tight against the end of the fingerboard. Make a pin from wire or a nail, leave the pin protrude above the neck a little way, and cut a notch in the nut to fit over this pin. It will not move sideways from the tension of the strings.

The slots for each set of strings should be less than ⅛ inch apart, and the slots should only be cut deep enough to accommodate the strings. A holder can be made to hold the nut while cutting the slots. To make a holder, rout a ¼ inch groove in the edge of a piece of wood. Slope the edge slightly with a rasp to match the slope of the nut. Clamp the holder to a bench while you are using it. See Fig. 3-25. The distance between the sets of strings should be equal. You can use a knife or saw to cut the slots in the strings.

**The Bridge.** Sound is created by vibrations. Therefore, the bridge should be made from hard wood. Hard wood will carry the vibrations from the strings into the mandolin body where they are produced into sound and magnified.

The style of the bridge should match the instrument. If you have achieved the proper tilt between the neck and body, the bridge

Fig. 3-25. The nut holder.

should be about ⅜ of an inch thick when finished. It should not be more than ¾ of an inch wide and about 4 inches long.

Cut the bridge from a piece of hard wood. This piece of wood should be long enough (to begin with) to be used on a table saw to cut the groove for the bridge saddle. The saw blade used to cut the groove for the bridge saddle should be about the same thickness as the saddle itself.

Sometimes I make my own bridge saddle. Also, I buy blank guitar bridge saddles and cut them to length. The bridge saddle can be made from the same material as the nut. It should fit snugly into the groove cut into the bridge.

Space the overall width of the strings to match the taper of the fingerboard. Cut the string slots in the saddle just deep enough for the strings. Space each string the same as you did for the nut except that each set of strings will be wider apart at the bridge. The outside strings should be about 3/32 of an inch from the edge of the fingerboard. For ease of playing, the strings must be the proper height from the frets.

At the nut end of the fingerboard, the strings should be high enough above the first fret so that a mandolin pick placed between the fret and string will remain there. At the last fret—that is toward the bridge—the string height over the fret should be about 5/32 of an inch. These heights are achieved by rasping and sanding the bottom side of the nut and bridge accordingly until the strings are the proper height.

After the proper string height has been achieved, remove the strings, keys, and tailpiece. You are ready to proceed with the binding and finishing. Refer to Chapters 11 and 12 on binding and finishing.

## STRINGING AND TUNING THE MANDOLIN

Allow maximum drying time for the finish. Reassemble the keys and tailpiece. Cut heavy paper to fit over the mandolin head. A paper punch can be used to punch holes in the paper to fit around the key pegs. The paper will keep the strings from scratching the finish. It will be removed after the strings are tuned.

### Stringing

In a package of mandolin strings, there are four envelopes. Each envelope contains two strings with the envelopes marked *E. A. D. G.* or numbered according to string gauge. Hold the mandolin in playing position with the back of the instrument held against your body and the neck in the left hand. The E, or smaller diameter string, will be the farthest string from you (after you have the mandolin strung up). This is the first string.

Looking closer to your body, the second, or A string, is next. This is followed by the D string. The string that is largest in size is G (the fourth string). Each double set of strings is tuned to the same note of the string as shown on the envelope. In other words, E is the first string, A is the second string, D is the third string, and G is the fourth string.

Taking one outside string at a time, hook the loop end over the proper hook made in the tailpiece. The other end of the string goes in the hole of the tuning peg. Make sure that it is wound around the pegs in such a manner that the string is on the inside of the peg next to the center of the head. Follow this procedure until all the strings have been put on the mandolin. Clip off the excess ends of the strings with wire cutters.

## Tuning

The G, or largest string, on the mandolin is tuned to the G note (lower than middle C). All other strings are tuned higher than middle C. A piano is better to tune from than a mandolin tuner. In tuning with the piano, you can find if the string is too high or too low much easier than with a tuner. And you will be less likely to break strings.

# Chapter 4

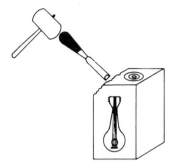

# A Mandolin Case

A mandolin case is easy to make. My case is shown in Fig. 2-5. It is made from ⅛-inch plywood. Corner moulding was used on the inside to form a framework. My case is 28 inches long. It is 12 inches wide at one end and 7¼ inches wide at the other end. It is 3½ inches thick.

To taper the front and back pieces, you must first cut two pieces of plywood 12 × 28 inches. Measure and mark one end of a piece at 7¼ inches. Draw a line from this mark to the corner on the other end of the piece. Cut this tapered piece off the side. See Fig. 4-1. The other piece must be cut in the same manner.

Cut two pieces of corner moulding 27¾ inches long. Miter both ends of each piece to a 45-degree angle. The moulding must be glued ⅛ of an inch in from the edges of each front and back piece.

Cut two pieces of moulding 7 inches long. Miter one end of each piece to a 45-degree angle. Because the other end is not square it must be hand fitted. Glue this piece at the narrow end of the front and back pieces. The 11¾ pieces at the other end must be cut and glued in the same way.

Cut plywood strips 1½ inches wide and glue around the other section to form sides. Plywood strips 2 inches wide must be glued around the other section to form sides for the other half of the case. Solid wood ¼ × ½ inches must be cut to fit and glued to the inside edge of the side pieces. In each corner of both sections, moulding must be cut and fit to each corner. Glue these pieces in place.

A neck rest made from a soft, solid wood must be cut and fitted around the corner moulding. The neck rest should be spaced about 7

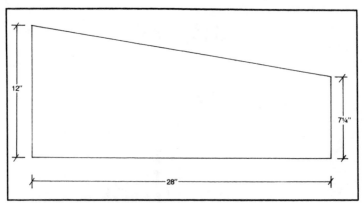

Fig. 4-1. The shape of a side piece for the mandolin case.

inches from the narrow end of the section that has 2 inch sides. A half-moon shaped place about 1 inch deep should be made in the edge for the neck to rest in.

In my garage, there was an abandoned hair dryer case. The hinges, catch, and handle were just what I needed for my case. These items must be obtained to use on the case.

The case should be lined inside with flannel or some other soft material. The lining can be glued to the wood. You can cover the outside of the case with contact paper or the case can be sanded, stained, and varnished. Similar cases can be made for a ukulele and a plucked dulcimer.

# Chapter 5

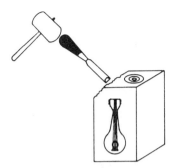

# Plucked Dulcimer

The dulcimer is one of the oldest musical instruments known to man. Many different sizes and shapes have been designed for the dulcimer. It is played by different methods. There is the dulcimer that is plucked or strummed and the dulcimer with strings that are hammered with a mallet. Some people declare that the piano is just a large dulcimer with strings that are hammered by pressing keys rather than the mallet being held in your hand. A dulcimer like the one shown in Fig. 2-9 is easy to make. There is no wood to bend and no curved saw cuts to make. This is an ideal instrument for the person to make who has only a few tools or who does not have the inclination to bend wood for the sides.

## MATERIALS

This instrument can be made from either ⅛-inch plywood or straight-grained wood. Two pieces of wood 10 × 30 inches will be needed for the front and back. The sides should be 2 inches wide and ¼ inch thick to provide gluing surface. It will take 6 feet of wood for the sides. If you are using plywood, you will need twice as much so that two pieces can be glued together to make ¼-inch thick sides.

The noting bar will be 1⅜ inches wide when the sides of the board have been sanded. It should be slightly longer than 30 inches to allow for squaring the ends. The noting bar on the instrument shown in Fig. 2-9 is ¾ inches thick. A noting bar of this thickness allows more freedom of action when playing the dulcimer than a fingerboard of lesser thickness.

A piece of wood ½ inch thick and 24 inches long will make both the head and tailpiece. The body of the dulcimer shown in Fig. 2-9 was made from cherry. The head and tailpiece are both made from tree of heaven wood.

## END AND CORNER BLOCKS

The end blocks can be laminated to gain the required thickness. Any kind of wood you have on hand will do. Nevertheless, they must be the same thickness as the sides. A piece of wood 2 × 2½ × 18 inches should be enough to make both end blocks and corner blocks.

## INSIDE BRACING

I prefer to use corner moulding for inside bracing. Nevertheless, you can use ⅜-×-½ inch strips of wood. Approximately 5 feet will be needed.

## ACCESSORIES

You will need one-half set of mandolin tuning pegs, three .012-gauge strings, and one .022-gauge string. The strings should be the ball-end type. You will also need 2½ feet of fret wire.

## THE WORKBOARD

The easiest and best way to make this dulcimer is on a workboard. Building it on a workboard will keep it straight and level. The corners are much easier to fit and glue on a workboard than by any other method. The thickness of the workboard is not a crucial factor. It must be smooth and level and not cupped or warped. The workboard should be 12 inches wide and 30 inches long.

Refer to Fig. 5-1. Mark the center at each end of the board and draw a center line the full length of the board. This line should be marked $A$ at each end. If the board is longer than 30 inches, measure and mark the board on the center line so that your layout will be just 30 inches. At 15 inches from one end, make a mark and label it $B$.

Use a square on the center line at B and mark a line vertical to the center line 4⅞ inches toward each side of the board. This is the B line. There is no B line shown in Fig. 5-1. At the end of this line (or 4⅞ inches from the center line) measure each way 5½ inches and draw another line. This is a $C$ line. Make a C line on each side of the workboard. Mark a $D$ at each end of both C lines. Check to make sure each C line is 11 inches long and exactly parallel or square with

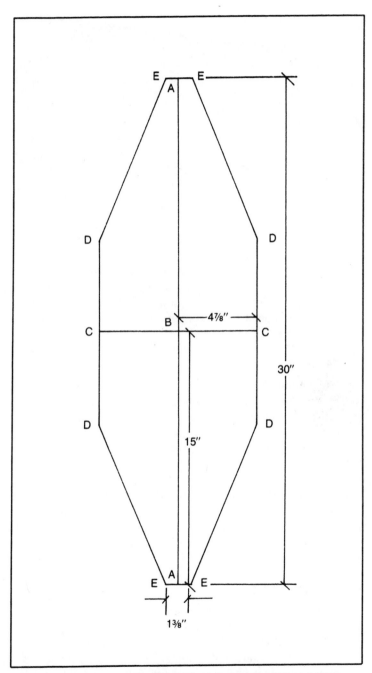

Fig. 5-1. A diagram of the workboard used in building a plucked dulcimer.

Fig. 5-2. Gluing the dulcimer.

the center line. The two C lines should be 9¾ inches apart. At each end of the center line, measure on both sides toward the edge of the board, mark the 11/16-inch point and mark *E*. These two marks shouid be 1⅜ inches apart. Draw a line from each E point to its corresponding D point on the corner of the board. Your workboard should look like Fig. 5-1.

## THE FRAMEWORK

**Side Supports.** Cover the workboard with waxed paper. Use a paper that the lines will show through. The purpose of the paper is to keep the sides from becoming glued to the workboard. The side supports should be at least 2 inches wide, ¾ of an inch thick, and 8 inches long. Use a C-clamp and attach a side support to each side of the workboard.

The side support should be placed along the C line on the outside toward the edge of the board. Be sure the supports are standing square with the board. See Fig. 5-2. The side supports are not a part of the framework of the dulcimer. The side pieces are held in place with a C-clamp to the side supports while they are fitted and glued together.

## CENTER SIDE PIECES

Cut two side pieces 2 inches wide and 11 inches long. Be sure the ends are cut square. These are center side pieces.

Attach one center side piece to each side support. These pieces go on the inside of the C line. Use C-clamps to hold these pieces to the side supports. Check Fig. 5-2.

## INSIDE BRACING

The purpose of the inside bracing is to give strength to the front and back and to prevent the instrument from becoming accidentally crushed. If you use corner moulding for bracing, simply cut it to length and cut and fit short pieces of wood in the ends so that the bracing itself is the same width as the sides. See Figs. 5-1 and 5-3. You should have on hand a good quality wood glue that is recommended for use by cabinetmakers. Glue the ends of the bracing to the side pieces. The bracing should be spaced about an inch from each end of the center side pieces.

## CORNER BLOCKS

The corner blocks are used to hold the side corner joints in place. These blocks must be carefully fitted. See Fig. 5-4 for the shape of the corner blocks. Because the block itself is only 2 inches or less in length, it is best and safest to make and shape each one on the end of a piece of wood several inches long before cutting to length.

To mark for cutting the corner block, hold a strip of wood that is the same width as the sides along the center side piece. Let it reach all the way to the bracing. Now mark both edges of the wood you are using for the corner block where it crosses the E line. Turn the

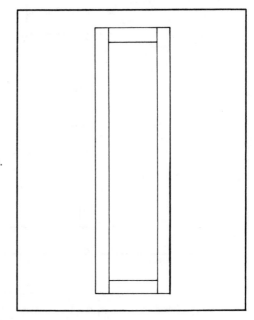

Fig. 5-3. Inside bracing.

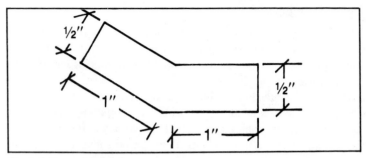

Fig. 5-4. Corner blocks.

piece of wood over and draw a line to those two marks and you are shown where to cut to get the angle for the corner block. Clamp the corner block to the side pieces.

## END BLOCKS

Figure 5-5 shows the shape of the end blocks. The sizes of the end blocks are 2 inches thick, the same as the sides. At the smallest end it is ⅞ inch tapered to 2¾ inches. Use a C-clamp and attach them to the workboard as shown in Fig. 5-2.

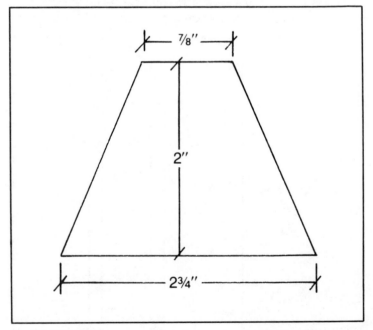

Fig. 5-5. End blocks.

## END SIDE PIECES

Cut four side pieces all the same length. Each side piece should be at least 11 inches long. Clamp the end blocks in position to the workboard. Place a side piece along each line from D to E. One end of each side piece must be cut on an angle to fit the center side piece already in place. With a saw and a rasp, work on each side piece until it fits perfectly at the corner joint. Use glue on each surface and glue the side pieces to the end and corner blocks. Use a C-clamp on the corner blocks. Be careful that there is no slippage leaving a gap in the joint. Clamp a piece of scrap wood to the board (as in Fig. 5-2) at the E end. The end side piece can be wedged between the end block and the scrap piece of wood. It is difficult to use a C-clamp at this position.

Allow the piece to set overnight and remove the glued-together side pieces from the workboard. Clean off the excess glue and waxed paper where it has stuck to the wood. You should now have a sturdy framework for the body of the dulcimer.

## THE TOP OF THE DULCIMER

What kind of wood are you using to make the dulcimer? Is it plywood or straight-grained wood? This chapter deals with the making of a dulcimer from plywood. If you decide to make the top and back from solid wood, refer to Chapter 10.

In the making of musical instruments, there are corner joints, sides, and ends of wood that are exposed. It is customary to use some sort of moulding to cover these exposed places.

Instrument makers use a binding around the edges of their instruments. The binding protects the edges from damage and makes a neater-looking instrument. A dulcimer made from straight-grained wood can be made without the use of binding. Read Chapter 8.

### Sanding the Underside of the Top

The plywood used for the top should be sanded on the underneath side. A few minutes work with a vibrator sander and coarse paper will remove at least 1/32 of wood. This makes the top thinner than the back. This allows for better vibration of the top. You will have a better-sounding instrument.

### Cutting the Top

After sanding the underside, cut the top piece of plywood into two 5-inch pieces. These two pieces will have a ¾-inch space

Fig. 5-6. Sound hole patterns: an angel pattern and a leaf pattern from a sweetheart ivy plant.

between them when glued to the framework. The noting bar will cover this space. You should now measure and mark the end blocks so that the ¾-inch space will be in the center of the framework.

## The Sound Holes

Many dulcimers have a sound hole made in the shape of a heart. I wanted to be different so I used an angel pattern for the sound hole in the dulcimer shown in Fig. 2-9. Patterns for two shaped sound holes are given in Fig. 5-6. The sound holes should be spaced and centered 15 inches from the end of the instrument and midway between the side and noting bar. Trace the pattern on the wood. Drill a starter hole. Use a sabre saw or any other tool you have to cut the sound holes.

## Gluing the Top to the Framework

It is best to hold the top sections in place on the framework and mark the top along the sides to give you a guide where to spread the glue. Cover the workboard with waxed paper. Place the two top sections on the waxed paper. Be sure to leave the ¾-inch space between the two sections. Spread the glue along the line on each top section. Also, spread glue on the framework. Do *not* glue the top to the inside bracing. Place the framework in position and weight it down. Be sure the weight is distributed evenly. Leave it overnight for the glue to dry.

If you are using binding on your dulcimer, you should study Chapter 11. The top must be routed for binding before you proceed in the construction of the dulcimer. Even without binding and if you are trimming the edge of the top with a router, the trimming must be done before gluing the noting bar. Refer to Chapter 11 for instructions on trimming the edges of the dulcimer with a router.

## THE NOTING BAR

The noting (pronounced note-ing) bar is sometimes called a sound bar, a fret board, or a fingerboard. Regardless of what it is called, the noting bar is where you play a tune on the dulcimer just as you use the keyboard of a piano to play a tune.

### Cutting the Noting Bar to Size

The noting bar should be made from a fairly hard wood. It must be straight. The noting bar on the dulcimer shown in Fig. 2-9 is ¾ of an inch thick. A bar of this thickness gives more finger room than one only ½ inch thick. The noting bar should be ¾ × 1⅜ × 30 inches. Cut the bar to this size and sand the topside and both edges.

### Cutting the Underside of the Noting Bar

As it is now, the noting bar is very rigid. If you cut out the underside, it will provide a sort of relaxation. Therefore, the bar will be more flexible to carry the string vibration into the top of the instrument.

Figure 5-7 shows this being done on a table saw. Figure 5-8 shows the end of the noting bar. Set the blade on the table saw to cut ½ inch deep. The fence should be set ¼ inch away from the blade.

Begin cutting at the head end of the bar. Cut only to the last fret. Make one cut and then move the fence over for another cut.

Fig. 5-7. The end of the noting bar.

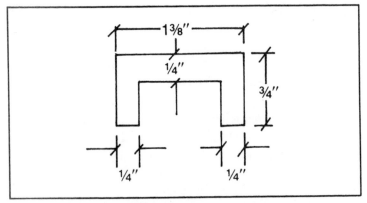

Fig. 5-8. The end of the noting bar after the underside has been cut out.

Proceed until you are within ¼ inch of the other side of the noting bar.

Lower the saw blade ⅛ of an inch and cut out the other end of the noting bar. You should have ¼ inch of wood left on three sides of the noting bar.

### Cutting the Saw Kerfs for Frets

You should have the fret wire on hand before attempting to saw the kerfs. Use the pattern in Fig. 5-9 to find the correct spacing for the frets. A fret saw can be purchased for this job or any thin-bladed saw will do. Nevertheless, the kerf should be no wider than .023. Use a miter box (as in Fig. 3-17) to make sure the kerfs are cut straight across the bar. Only cut deep enough for the frets to be seated properly.

Size and shape are not too important in a musical instrument. What is crucial is the string length between the nut and bridge. Proper fret spacing is also necessary. If the fret spacing does not match the string length, the instrument will not sound right.

Figure 5-10 shows a space cut in the noting bar between the last fret and bridge position. This is a picking space or strumming

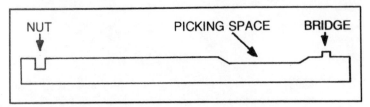

Fig. 5-9. Fret spacing for the plucked dulcimer.

space. The picking space should be about 3 inches long and centered between the bridge position and the last fret. The picking space should be ⅛ of an inch deep. It can be cut out on a band saw, dado heads, or simply made with hand tools. Slope the ends of the cut so it will look neat.

The nut is a piece of wood that has string slots cut in it. The strings ride over this piece of wood and are held in place. Because the nut is a permanent fixture on a dulcimer, it must be fastened in place.

A notch 3/16 of an inch wide and ⅛ inch deep is cut square across the noting bar. Refer to Fig. 5-10 and measure the exact spot for the nut. When you are ready to set the nut in place, spot glue it in the notch.

### Installing the Frets

Refer to Fig. 3-8. I have an iron block that I use to lay the board on while I set the frets. Any solid place will do for this. Preferably, you should use a corner of a table over the leg. A brass hammer should be used. An iron hammer used to set the frets must have a smooth head. A pitted hammer head will damage and mar frets.

### Filing the Fret Ends

Clamp a block of wood to the table as shown in Fig. 3-8. Hold the bar against the block of wood and file the ends of the frets until they are smooth and even with the bar. When all the fret ends have been filed, hold the bar along the edge of the table and file along the edge of the bar. See Fig. 3-9. Hold the file so the fret ends will be tapered inward. Crocus cloth can be used after filing to remove any sharp places on the ends of the frets.

### GLUING

Place the partially completed instrument on the table. Spread glue to the top along edges of the open space. Spread glue on edges of noting bar. Clamp the bar at each end to the end blocks. Turn the

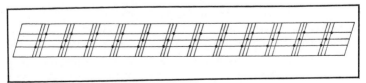

Fig. 5-10. The noting bar showing the nut, bridge, and picking space.

Fig. 5-11. The head of a dulcimer.

instrument over with the bar on the table. Block under edges of the instrument so it will not topple over. Weight the top down to the noting bar with bricks or any kind of suitable weights. Allow the pieces to set overnight.

Rubber bands or weights can be used to hold the back in place while the glue sets. Be sure to glue the back to the inside bracing.

Each end of the dulcimer must be cut off square. The easiest way to do this is on a radial arm saw. Nevertheless, it can be done with hand tools.

## THE HEAD

The dulcimer shown in Fig. 2-6 has a violin-type head and tuning pegs. A head of this type is easy to make. The trouble lies in the friction tuning pegs. The peg is tapered to fit a tapered hole. Even if the pegs fit perfectly, an instrument of this type is difficult to tune and easily slips out of tune.

The dulcimer shown in Fig. 2-9 has mandolin machine heads for tuners. There is no trouble at all tuning the dulcimer with this type of keys. Therefore, I have given instructions for making the dulcimer head including the use of mandolin keys. Figure 5-11 shows the head on the instrument with the keys and strings attached.

Figure 5-12 illustrates the head. The head and heel were made from tree of heaven wood. The size of the head is ½ × 2 × 6½ inches. You will do well to use a piece of wood longer than 6½ inches for the head. This allows extra wood for trimming the ends.

Glue together enough pieces of the same kind of wood to obtain the required thickness for the heel. To figure the necessary thick-

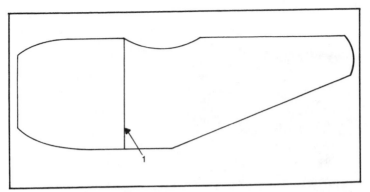

Fig. 5-12. A dulcimer head.

ness, the head and heel must be measured from the top of the noting bar to the back of the dulcimer.

See Fig. 5-13 for gluing the head and heel. The wood for the heel is glued on at arrow 1 of Fig. 5-12 or 4½ inches from the tip of the head. The heel should be tapered back to within 1 inch of the end of the instrument. The front part of the heel should be rounded.

A template such as shown in Fig. 3-23 should be used when drilling for the keys. The head should slope downward from the body of the dulcimer. Cut the head on a radial arm saw to fit the body. Using a ½-inch block of wood between the tip end of the head and the saw fence will cause the head to be trimmed at the proper angle.

## THE TAILPIECE

Figure 5-14 shows the tailpiece. The tailpiece should be made from the same wood as the head. It should be ½ inch thick and wide

Fig. 5-13. Gluing the heel to the head.

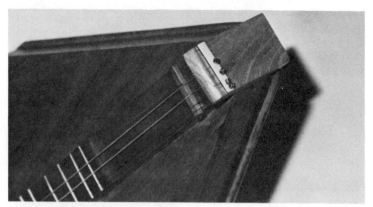

Fig. 5-14. The tailpiece on a dulcimer.

enough to cover the tail end of the instrument. The tailpiece should be ½ inch higher than the noting bar.

The holes for the strings should enter the wood close to the noting bar and be drilled through the tailpiece at a downward angle. Ivoroid binding should be used to keep the ends of the strings from penetrating into the wood. Five string holes should be drilled.

The dulcimer is held on your lap or on a table for playing. The head is at the player's left. Two holes about ⅛ of an inch apart for the melody strings should be drilled in the side of the tailpiece that will be closest the player's body. The remaining distance should be divided so three more holes can be drilled. This method of drilling allows you to have two melody and two drone strings. Or you can use one melody and three drone strings.

Figure 5-15 shows long clamps being used to glue the head and tailpiece to the dulcimer. If clamps are used, glue the tailpiece on before gluing the head.

It is possible to use block and wedges, as shown in Fig. 5-2, to glue the head and tailpiece. You must be careful in using either method to keep the head in proper alignment.

### THE NUT AND THE BRIDGE

The nut should be made from hard wood. It should be 3/16 of an inch thick and 5/16 of an inch high. Cut string slots in the nut to match the string holes in the tailpiece.

The bridge should be ¼ inch wide and ¼ inch high. Cut string slots in the bridge to match the string holes in the tailpiece.

Install the keys and strings. Sand the bottom of the nut and bridge to get the proper string height. The string height at the fret closest the nut should not be more than 1/16 inch. At the fret closest the bridge, the string height should be no higher than 5/32 inch. If you can get the strings lower than this without rattling on the frets, your dulcimer will be easier to play.

Remove the strings, bridge and keys. Spot glue the nut in place. You are ready to bind, sand, and finish your dulcimer.

## TUNING

The dulcimer is normally tuned to the key of C. The string farthest from the body when the dulcimer is held in playing position is tuned to the middle C note. All other strings are tuned to the G note (the G note higher than middle C).

If you want to make a dulcimer with curved sides, a pattern for the form is shown in Fig. 5-16. A form should be made in the shape of the dulcimer. The side pieces are then bent and shaped to the form. Instructions are given in Chapter 3 showing how to soak plywood and bend it to the shape of the dulcimer.

The side pieces must be lined with narrow strips of plywood to provide gluing surface for the top and back. The side pieces should be held in place on the form with clamps while the lining is glued in place. Do not use lining at the ends where the end blocks will be. This prevents the side pieces from losing their shape. Spring-type clothespins are handy to hold the lining to the side pieces while gluing.

End blocks (as in Fig. 5-5) must be used at each end of the dulcimer. A block of this size must be used. The block might need a slightly different taper to fit the curved side pieces.

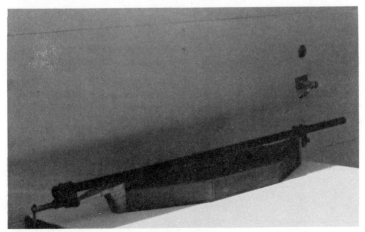

Fig. 5-15. Gluing the head to a dulcimer.

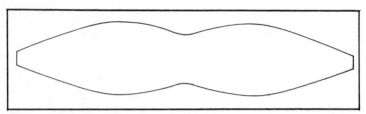

Fig. 5-16. The shape of the form to be used in making the curved sides of a dulcimer.

After the lining and end blocks have been glued, the back of the dulcimer can be glued to the side pieces. This should be done while the side pieces are held to the form with clamps. After the glue dries remove from the form.

The two top pieces should be glued to the noting bar and then glued in place on the instrument. Proceed with the head and tail-piece.

# Chapter 6

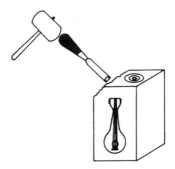

# Ukulele

The making of a ukulele is similar to the making of a mandolin. The starting place in making a ukulele is with the fingerboard. You can buy a ready-made fingerboard for a ukulele. Those I have seen were made from plastic and were fastened to the neck with screws. These fingerboards are one piece. The frets and the nut were formed along with the board. If you are buying the fingerboard, have it on hand before cutting out the neck. A fingerboard you buy might have a slightly different width than my pattern.

Figure 6-1 shows a pattern of the fingerboard used on the ukulele shown in Fig. 2-10. You can use the pattern and make your own fingerboard. Your ukulele will look more handmade. Follow the instructions in Chapter 3 to make the fingerboard.

The fingerboard used on the ukulele was made from chestnut. The neck was made from maple. Plywood was used for the sides and back. The nut was made from walnut. The bridge and top were made from mahogany. It is a nice little instrument.

### THE NECK

The piece of wood for the neck should be at least $1 \times 2 \times 13\frac{1}{2}$ inches long. A piece of wood 1 inch thick will allow the head to slope down $\frac{1}{2}$ inch.

Use the neck pattern shown in Fig. 6-2 to mark off the neck. Cut out the neck according to the front view shown in Fig. 6-3. Then glue two pieces of the 1-inch board to the heel end of the neck so it will be thick enough to form the heel.

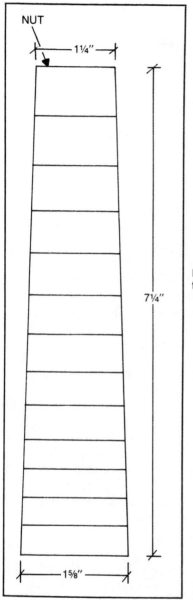

NUT

1¼"

7¼"

1⅝"

Fig. 6-1. The pattern for a ukulele fingerboard.

These pieces of wood must be planed or sanded smooth before gluing so the glue joints will not be so noticeable. The neck at the heel should be about 3 inches thick. This will allow the body of the ukulele to be about 3 inches thick.

After the heel portion of the neck has been glued, you will know how wide the side pieces will be. You can cut out sides and begin bending them while the glue on the neck joint sets. Then the neck can be worked down with a rasp while the sides soak, band, and dry.

## MARKING FOR THE SHAPE OF THE HEEL

The neck should be squared and cut off 13 inches from the head. Mark the center of the neck from one end to the other. Extend the mark completely down the neck end and across the bottom of the heel. The lower edge of the heel where the back of the ukulele will be glued should be wider than 1 inch.

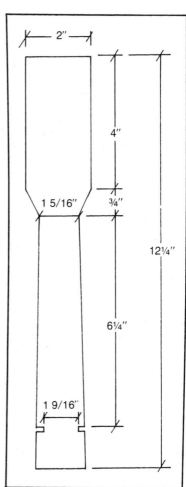

Fig. 6-2. The front view of a ukulele neck.

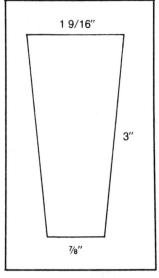

Fig. 6-3. The side view of a ukulele neck.

The heel of the neck is tapered down from the width of the fingerboard to 1 inch (or less) width at the bottom edge. Figure 6-4 shows the taper of the heel.

Much care should be taken in shaping the heel. Make it something you will be proud for others to see.

## THE FORM

A form will have to be made to bend the sides. There is a pattern for a form shown in Fig. 6-5. This pattern is for one side only. You can make a form just the shape of the pattern and it will do the job or you can cut the pattern out and make a full-sized form. Holes must be cut in the form to hook the clamps in.

The form shown in Fig. 6-6 was made from three pieces of Masonite siding with wood strips used between the pieces of siding. This gave me the width I needed and, because it is not solid, there is a space for air to circulate. Therefore, drying time was shortened. The center of the form should be marked at each end as a guide where to place the end of the sides for bending.

## THE SIDES

The top of the ukulele must be recessed into the neck so that it will be flush and even to allow the fingerboard to lap over the top. This must be taken into consideration when measuring for the width of the sides.

The top of the instrument should be no more than ⅛ inch thick (less if you can get it thinner). If the heel is 3 inches from top to bottom, the sides should only be cut 2⅞ inches wide.

I used two pieces for the sides of the ukulele, shown in Fig. 2-10, rather than one full-length piece. These two pieces were joined together at the end block. The length of the sides for the ukulele is 28¾ inches. It is easier to bend a piece of wood only half that long.

A full-length piece of side wood should be cut in half. Mark the cut ends. When bending the side pieces, bend them so the marked ends will fit together at the end block.

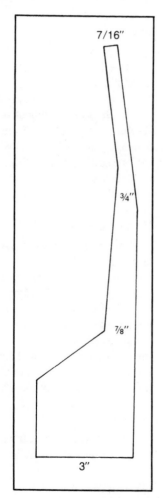

Fig. 6-4. The taper of a ukulele heel.

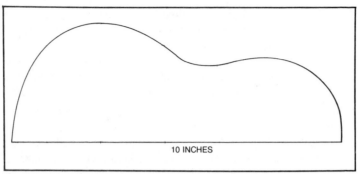

Fig. 6-5. One side of the form used to bend ukulele sides.

### Bending the Sides

Refer to Chapter 3 and especially the section on bending the sides. The same method of soaking and bending the sides for a mandolin will be used in bending the sides of a ukulele.

The mandolin sides are bent in more or less a circle. The sides of a ukulele must be bent in two different directions—in and out. Ukulele sides are much more difficult to bend than those for a mandolin. Work the wood with your hands after it has been soaked (before putting it on the form). Be sure the wood is pliable so it will not crack or break when bending it around the form. Figure 6-6 shows the side piece in the form.

### Lining the Sides

After the side piece has dried, the clamps should be loosened and the side pieces should be moved upward in the form about an inch. Insert waxed paper between the side piece and the form. This will prevent the sides from becoming glued to the form.

Tighten the clamps and glue strips of ⅛-inch plywood to the inside edge of the side piece to provide a gluing surface for the top and back. After the glue dries, the side piece can be removed from the form and it will hold its shape while the other edge is lined. The same procedure is used in making the other side piece. In Fig. 6-6, the side piece in the form has the lining clamped in place.

### The End Block

If it is available, soft wood should be used for the end block. A soft wood is easy to work with.

The end block should be as long as the sides are wide and at least 3 inches wide. The sides should be placed on a table and held in position while the shape of the end block is determined. The end block must be made to fit the slight curve of the tail end of the side pieces. After the end block has been shaped, the side pieces should be glued to the end block.

## Cutting Slots in the Neck for the Sides

A slot must be cut in each side of the neck for the sides. The sides are glued in the slots. Refer to Fig. 3-10 before cutting the slots in the neck. The slots on the ukulele neck should be cut straight into the neck and about ¼ inch deep.

When the top is glued on the neck it must be even with the top of the fingerboard. A portion of the neck must be cut away to allow the top to be recessed. From the neck slots to the end of the neck, cut with a saw or rasp until the recessed place is ⅛ of an inch deep.

## Gluing the Sides

Figure 3-12 shows a mandolin neck and sides being glued together. The instructions for gluing the mandolin apply to the ukulele. Be sure to use a strip of plywood at the tail end of the instrument to keep the sides even with the top of the neck.

Blocks of wood must be cut and fitted and glued in place between the neck and sides. These blocks of wood keep the sides from separating from the neck. Figure 3-13 shows these blocks as wedge shaped inside the body of the mandolin.

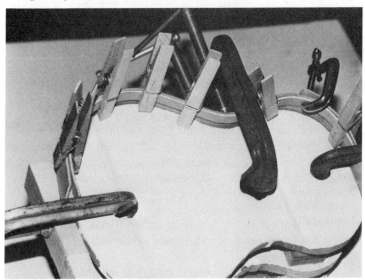

Fig. 6-6. The form for bending ukulele sides.

## THE TOP

A straight-grained wood top can be made for the ukulele. See Chapter 10.

A plywood top can be sanded on the underneath side. As much as 1/32 of an inch can be sanded away. The top should be marked on the inside of the side pieces and the portion between the marks sanded. The full ⅛ of an inch will be left to glue to the side pieces. When gluing the top to the instrument, do not use clamps. Use weights to hold the top while gluing.

If you are using binding on the ukulele, the groove for the binding must be routed before additional work is done to the instrument. See Chapter 11.

Unless you have a clamp with a deep throat to reach the bridge through the sound hole, the bridge must be glued on before the back of the ukulele. If such a clamp is available, the instrument can be completed and then the bridge can be made and glued on.

## THE BRIDGE, NUT, AND PEGS

**The Pegs.** The holes for the tuning pegs should be drilled. Drill the holes the size the pegs will fit snugly. A template is not necessary. The spacing of the pegs in the head should be uniform. The fingerboard should be made and glued to the neck before making the nut and bridge.

**The Nut.** The nut should be 3/16 of an inch thick. It must be high enough so that the strings will clear the first fret by 1/16 of an inch.

The ukulele has four strings. The outside strings should be spaced ⅛ of an inch in from the edge of the fingerboard. The distance between the outside strings should be equally spaced for the two remaining strings. Cut grooves in the nut to hold the strings.

**The Bridge.** The base of the bridge on the ukulele, shown in Fig. 2-10 is 1¼ inches wide. It is 3¼ inches long. The bridge was made this size to provide plenty of gluing surface. The top of the bridge is ⅜ × 2⅛ inches. The bridge you make for your ukulele should be similar in size.

The bridge on the ukulele is shaped similar to the mandolin bridge. Figure 6-7 shows a ukulele bridge. Figure 6-8 shows the ends of the bridge being shaped. Figure 6-9 shows a cross section of the bridge.

After the bridge has been shaped, you must determine how high it will be. Attach pegs in the peg holes nearest the nut. Attach

Fig. 6-7. The bridge of a ukulele.

two strings (or fine wire) to the pegs. Stretch the strings across the nut to the bridge position.

The string clearance at the first fret should be less than 1/16 of an inch. At the last fret, the string clearance is less than ⅛ of an inch. From this you can judge about what the bridge height should be. After the top of the bridge has been sanded, use the bridge itself to make the fine adjustment in the string height.

After the bridge height has been achieved, hold the bridge in position and mark for the string holes. Fret wire can be used along the front edge of the bridge for a saddle.

Figure 6-7 shows how the holes are drilled at an angle through the bridge.

### Gluing the Bridge

Cut out a block of wood the same size as the base of the bridge and ¼ of an inch thick. Drill two small holes in the bottom of the bridge. These holes should be between the strings—not under them. Use wires in these holes and let the wires protrude a short way from the wood. Use two strings in the outside string holes and attach the other end to the pegs.

Hold the bridge so the saddle will be 13½ inches from the nut. Move the bridge sideways until the strings line up with the edge of the fingerboard. When the strings are lined up perfectly, press the bridge down and the wires will mark the top.

Before removing the wires from the bridge, press the wires down on the ¼-inch block of wood and mark it for drilling. Remove the wires from the bridge.

Drill ¼-inch holes in the bridge in the exact spot where the wire markers were. Drill only part way through the bridge.

Drill ¼-inch holes through the top and the ¼-inch block. Use ¼-inch dowels in these holes. You are actually pinning the bridge to the block inside the instrument under the top.

Glue the dowels in the bridge, the top, and the block. Glue the bridge to the top and the block of wood underneath the top. The

Fig. 6-8. Shaping the ends of the bridge with a rasp.

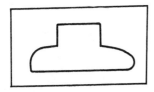

Fig. 6-9. A cross section of a ukulele bridge.

bridge will not come off. Use clamps or weights to hold the bridge assembly in place while the glue sets.

## THE SOUND HOLE

The sound hole should be 2 inches in diameter. Center the sound hole under the strings between the fingerboard and bridge.

A ukulele top made from plywood needs no bracing. A top made from straight-grained wood must be braced around the sound hole. It should have one strip of bracing all the way across the top near the bridge.

Glue on the back and you are ready for the binding. See Chapters 11 and 12.

# Chapter 7

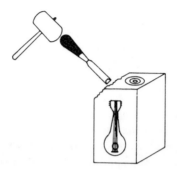

# Hammered Dulcimer

The hammered dulcimer is so unlike its sister, the plucked dulcimer, that it is a mystery why the instruments have such similar names. Perhaps it is because they both make sweet (dulcet) music. But that is something almost all instruments do.

The body of the dulcimer shown in Fig. 2-11 was made completely from poplar. The bracing and pin blocks were made from a hard wood. The poplar was all ½ of an inch thick. Building an instrument out of wood this thick gives you an opportunity to use your imagination and use wood of different shades. A combination of different shades of wood will enhance the appearance of your dulcimer. Some of the most popular woods used in building a hammered dulcimer are cherry, maple, walnut, chestnut, mahogany, and poplar.

My son worked with me in making this dulcimer. We wanted the dulcimer to be 16 × 33 inches (outside measurements). The poplar for the top and back was about 40 inches long and ¾ of an inch thick. We glued the pieces together to make the top and back. After gluing, the width was 18 inches. After the glue set, the two pieces were run through a commercial planer and planed to ½ inch. We used ½-×-3 inch poplar for the sides. This was all the wood we needed for the outside of the instrument.

## TAPERING THE SIDE PIECES

We ripped the end pieces to 2½ inches so our dulcimer is 2½ inches thick at the ends and 3 inches at the center.

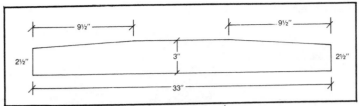

Fig. 7-1. The tapered ends of side pieces for a hammered dulcimer.

The soundboard on this dulcimer is not square; it is 14 × 23 × 15 inches. Look again at Fig. 2-11. See the shape of the top? The side pieces must be tapered to make the dulcimer this shape. The side pieces must be cut so they are both exactly 33 inches long. Figures 7-1 and 7-2 show how the side pieces look after they have been tapered.

The ends of the side pieces will be 2½ inches wide. Mark the ends at 2½ inches and cut the taper to 4 ½ inches from each end on one side piece and 9½ inches on the other side piece. Thus the soundboard will be 14 × 23 × 15 inches. The end panels of the top will each be ½ inch lower at the ends of the dulcimer than the sound top.

## MITERING THE SIDE PIECES

We mitered the ends of the side pieces on a table saw. The blade was tilted to a 45-degree angle. The corners of this instrument do not have to be mitered. They can be left square. If you decide to miter the corners on your dulcimer, the end pieces must be cut exactly 16 inches long. If you do not miter, they will be cut only 15 inches in length.

The back for the dulcimer was cut 15 × 32 inches square and fit inside the sides of the dulcimer.

## BUILDING THE SIDES

We did not use clamps when we glued the sides to the back. The side pieces were held in place by hand. Small nails were used to

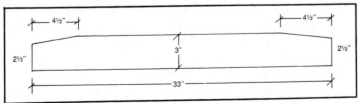

Fig. 7-2. The tapered ends of side pieces for a hammered dulcimer.

Fig. 7-3. The inside of a hammered dulcimer.

hold the wood together while the glue set. Enough of the nail heads were left protruding from the wood to grasp and remove with pliers. The nails were removed before sanding. After finishing, wood screws with finishing washers were used in the nail holes. The screws and finishing washers add an extra touch to this type of instrument.

Gluing clamps can be used to hold the side pieces. If you use clamps, a piece of wood such as a 2 × 4 should be used between the clamps and the side pieces. This will cause the clamping pressure to be evenly distributed.

## PIN BLOCKS

Mark again the ends of the side pieces. On one side piece, the mark is 4½ inches from each end. On the other side the mark is 9½ inches from each end. The soundboard fits within these marks. The pin blocks fit between these marks and the end of the instrument.

One pin block will have pins set in it to hold the strings. The other pin block will have the tuning pins set in it. The instrument has 36 strings. The pin blocks must be made of hard, solid wood. They must be well braced to withstand the pressure of the strings. In addition, the wood must be hard so that, as the tuning pins are turned, they do not wear the wood away and become loose.

In measuring for the thickness of the pin blocks, you must allow for the thickness of the top. Figure 7-3 shows the pin blocks and the bracing glued in place. Figure 7-4 shows an end view of a pin block. It must be tapered to fit the slope cut on the end of the side pieces.

The ends of the blocks must be measured and cut at an angle. Because the pin blocks are not placed square across the instrument, the ends of the blocks must be cut to fit. Also, we cut each corner of the pin block square so the bracing would fit against the squared-off corner.

Glue the blocks to the back and sides of the instrument.

## BRACING THE PIN BLOCKS

In Fig. 7-3, the 1-inch piece of wood you see glued to each side piece between the pin blocks serves two purposes: the soundboard rests on these pieces, and this is the pin block bracing. A soft wood will *not* do for this bracing. It must be a hard, solid wood. The bracing you see in Fig. 7-3 is a full 1 inch thick. Glue the bracing to the back, the sides, and the pin blocks.

## THE TOP

The wood for the top must be glued up the same as the back. The top on the dulcimer shown in Fig. 2-11 was made from ½-inch poplar.

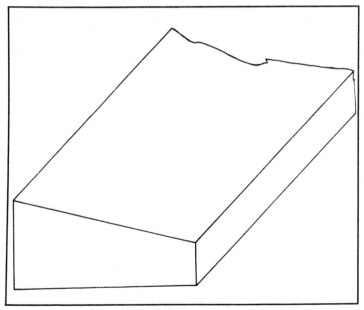

Fig. 7-4. The end view of a pin block.

Fig. 7-5. Using a guide for the power saw to cut out the soundboard.

The top is made in three sections (the end top pieces and the soundboard). The soundboard is cut in a square trapezoidal shape. The soundboard measures 14 × 23 × 15 inches.

The soundboard should be cut out of the center of the piece of wood you glued for the top. It is cut out of the center; the remainder of the wood on each end will make the top end pieces. The grain of the wood will match.

First rip the top on a table saw so that it will fit snugly between the side pieces of the instrument. Lay off the soundboard to the dimensions given above. Clamp a straight piece of wood on the top to act as a guide and cut the soundboard with a powersaw. My son demonstrates this technique in Fig. 7-5.

## THE SOUND HOLES

We used the drill press and a 2½-inch hole saw to cut the sound holes. See Fig. 3-16.

The sound holes were centered 6¾ inches from the narrow side of the sound board. There is a 3⅛-inch separation between the holes. This is a good-looking spacing for the sound holes. See Fig. 2-11.

The soundboard does not rest on the pin blocks. It rests on the pieces of wood glued on the soundbox side of the pin block. A piece of wood should be glued to the pin blocks for the ends of the soundboard to rest on.

The end top panels will not be level with the soundboard. The top panels turn down at each end according to the taper cut on the side pieces. This means that the end of each panel must be beveled to fit against the soundboard.

We beveled these top pieces on a table saw. A power saw can be used with the table tilted to the proper angle. A guide clamped to the board for the edge of the saw base is necessary. The end panels must be beveled to fit against the soundboard before cutting them to length.

A support must be cut to the proper thickness and glued to the end pieces for the end top pieces to rest on. There should be a block of wood glued to the inside of the side pieces between the pin block and the end of the instrument. This will prevent the top from sagging. To keep the soundboard from sagging, a post must be glued in place in the center of the sound box.

The top of a hammered dulcimer need not be glued to the body. You can glue the top, but screws and finishing washers will serve as well.

## BRIDGES

A hammered dulcimer has three bridges: the end bridges nearest the pins and a center bridge.

We made the bridges for the dulcimer, shown in Fig. 2-11, out of maple. The bridge saddles were made from ⅛-inch brass welding rod. The groove for the bridge saddle was cut with a router.

A guide was clamped to the board from which the bridges were made. The router was held against the guide while the groove for the bridge saddle was cut. The groove can be cut on a table saw by using a thin blade.

The bridges were cut out on the table saw after the saddle grooves were routed. The two end bridges are ⅜ of an inch wide at

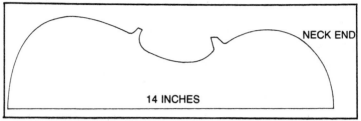

Fig. 7-6. A pattern for drilling pin holes.

the top, ⅝ of an inch wide at the base and ⅜ of an inch high. The center bridge is ⅜ of an inch at the top, ¾ of an inch at the base and ¾ of an inch high. The groove for the bridge saddle is right in the center of the ⅜ inch top. This makes for nice-looking bridges.

The saw was tilted the correct angle to cut the bridging to the preferred shape.

## THE PINS

The player sits at the wide side of the soundboard in the playing position. The tuning pins are at the players right.

A template is necessary when drilling the holes for the pins. A pattern is shown in Fig. 7-6 for the pin spacing. The holding pins must be set in the wood at an angle. If the pins are set straight in the pin block, the strings will slip up and off the pins. The wood for the template must be at least ¾ of an inch thick. The pattern should be taped to the wood and the pin holes marked with an awl.

Tack a ¼-×-¼ strip of wood to one edge of the template before drilling the holes in the template with a drill press. This strip of wood will be used on the edge of the template next to the end of the dulcimer. This will cause the holes to be drilled at an angle.

The tuning pins will likely require a 3/16-inch diameter hole. The string holding pins can be made from ⅛-inch brass welding rod or you can use 3/16-inch rods. To use the ⅛-inch rods, you must drill the holes for these pins in the pin block, and then ream the holes in the template to the proper size to drill for the tuning pins.

When the holes have been drilled in the template, remove the strip of wood. Clamp the template to the instrument and drill the pin holes with a hand drill.

The holding pins can be driven in place. There should be at least ½ inch of each pin protruding above the top of the instrument.

When you purchase the tuning pins, you will need to order a tuning pin key. The tuning pins are not driven in the pins holes; they are turned in with the key.

## THE STRINGS

The hammered dulcimer has 12 sets of strings. Each set has three strings. You should use two plain strings, .014 to .016 in diameter, and one .022 to .024 wound string in each set. The plain strings in each set will be located nearest the player as he sits in playing position. The strings must be the loop-end type. The loop on the end of the string hooks over the holding pins.

It is possible to use piano wire and make a loop on each string. To make the loop, a nail should be driven completely through a short board. Clamp the board to a table in such a manner that the nail is projecting over the table edge a few inches.

About 4 inches from the end of the piano wire, bend the wire around the nail. Twist the end of the wire around the string by hand. Make a few loops for practice before actually beginning to make the loops on the strings.

## THE HAMMERS

A piano is played by pressing the keys. There is a knee-action mechanism that connects the keys to hammers that strike the strings causing them to vibrate. This creates sound.

The strings of the hammered dulcimer vibrate when struck with hammers held by hand. This is why it is called a hammered dulcimer. The hammers should be made from hard wood. The hammers shown with the instrument in Fig. 2-11 were made from walnut. A pattern for hammers is given in Fig.7-7. You can style your own hammers. Those shown with the instrument have a stiff handle. You might want to use a thinner handle so that it will be more flexible.

## TUNING

On any stringed instrument, the sounding length of the strings is important. On fretted instruments, the player presses the string down near the frets and shortens the sounding length of the string. When the string is plucked while it is pressed down on the fret, the note sounded is higher than when the string is plucked open or full

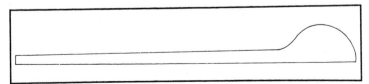

Fig. 7-7. A pattern for hammers for playing the hammered dulcimer.

length. This fretting of the string to play the higher note is only temporary.

The bridge positions on the hammered dulcimer are permanent. The sounding length of the strings remain fixed.

Your hammered dulcimer has three bridges. One is at each end of the strings near the pins and the other is positioned between the outer bridges. The center bridge is not positioned in the exact center of the strings. It is off center toward the holding pins. This causes the notes that are played on one side of the instrument to be higher than those played on the other side. The bridge positions given here should cause the notes played on the left side of the instrument to be four whole steps higher on the musical scale than those played on the right side.

On the side of the dulcimer that has the longest strings, the outside bridges should be 23 inches apart. The center bridge should be 8⅞ inches from the bridge on the left side. This gives two sounding lengths (of the first string) of 8⅞ and 14⅛ inches.

The outside bridges at the shortest strings should be 15⅝ inches. The center bridge is positioned 6⅛ inches from the left bridge. The sounding length will be 6⅛ and 9½ inches.

These measurements are approximate. You will need to make fine adjustments in the bridge settings.

You can tune your hammered dulcimer with the piano. Tune the first set of strings to the G note (below middle C) and tune the remaining strings, in order, right up the G scale. This will give you one sharp on the right playing side (F Sharp). All three strings in each set are tuned to the same note.

# Chapter 8

# Guitar

Before you begin to make a guitar, you should become well acquainted with Chapter 3. Many of the instructions needed for making the guitar will be found there. The guitar shown in Fig. 2-12 was used for the plans described in this book. The neck was made from Hondorus mahogany. The top was made from sitka spruce. The sides are plywood and the back is Philippine mahogany. The guitar has a walnut fingerboard and bridge.

## THE NECK

The neck for the guitar must be made from a hard, straight-grained wood. Hondorus mahogany makes a good neck. The next guitar I make I want to use a laminated neck. One piece will be maple and two pieces will be walnut. Any good, hard wood can be used to make a neck (especially if it is steel reinforced).

Before the neck is cut out on a band saw, you must plan for the reinforcement. The pull of the strings have a tendency to bend a guitar neck. A guitar neck made from vertical-grained wood might not bend and might not need reinforcement. Figure 8-1 shows an end cut of vertical-grained wood.

For a test, take a piece of wood about 2 feet long and about 1 inch square and see how much more rigid the wood is when you attempt to bend it against the grain. Be selective in choosing the wood for the neck. A neck made from a piece of wood picked off the lumber stack is more apt to bend than it is to remain straight.

Different kinds of reinforcement are used in guitar necks:

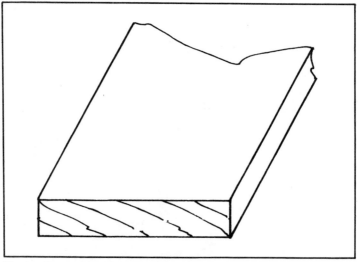

Fig. 8-1. The end cut of vertical-grained wood.

☐ Adjustable steel bar.
☐ A steel T-bar.
☐ A steel box bar.

Either one of the last two, properly installed, should keep a neck straight. Adjustable steel rod is installed when the guitar is built and is designed to straighten the neck after it has become bowed or warped. The guitar shown in Fig. 2-12 has an adjustable rod in the neck. Figure 8-2 shows the neck with rod glued in place.

The adjustable rod must be placed in the neck so the nut, by which the rod is turned, can be reached. The nut on the rod will not be covered with the fingerboard.

The piece of wood for the neck should be at least 23 inches long. It should be wide enough so that the peg head will be 3 inches wide when finished and at least 1 inch thick.

The groove for the reinforcement should be cut in the wood before the neck is cut out on the band saw. A router or table saw can be used to cut the groove.

Lay off the neck (see Fig. 8-3). Rout the groove for the reinforcement. Cut the neck out with a band saw. Figure 8-4 shows the side view of the neck. The head must turn down from the neck to cause the strings to fit properly on the nut. Some people like a lot of angle in the head while others like less. You must decide how much of an angle you want on the head.

If the wood you are using for the neck is not thick enough to get as much angle on the head as you prefer, a piece of wood can be glued to the underside of the peg head. This must be done, however, before any cutting is done with the band saw.

Figure 3-4 shows how an extra piece of wood is glued to the neck to make it thick enough for the angle of the peg head. In cutting the neck, it must be laid off according to the size of the fingerboard. Study the section on fingerboards before starting the neck.

**Shaping the Neck.** Use whatever tools you have to shape the neck; information is given in Chapter 3. I have made a number of necks just with a wood rasp after the neck was cut to rough shape on the band saw.

A guitar neck made from vertical-grained wood can be made thinner than other necks. If the neck is steel reinforced it can be made thinner. Some necks are made as thin as 7/16 of an inch. I would rather have a neck a little large and strong than a thin neck that bends.

If the wood for the neck is close, vertical grained, the thickness of the neck under the fingerboard should not be less than ½ of an inch at the narrow end. Make a gradual taper in the thickness of the neck until where the curve begins for the heel. The neck will be about ⅞ of an inch thick.

The underside of the neck should be well rounded to make for ease of playing the guitar.

## THE HEEL

A block of wood must be glued to the heel end of the neck. The heel must be glued up so that it is the same thickness as the sides

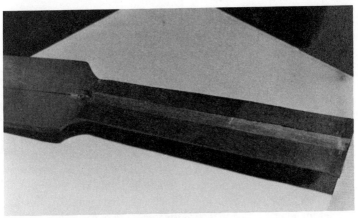

Fig. 8-2. A guitar neck with an adjustable rod glued in.

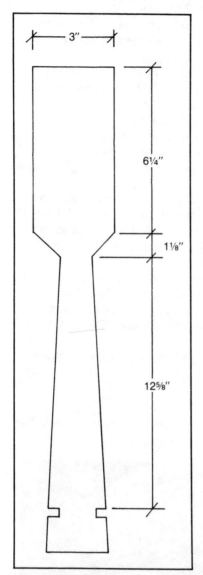

Fig. 8-3. The front view of a guitar neck.

will be wide (less the thickness of the top that will be recessed in neck). This is necessary so that the top will be even with the neck.

If at all possible, the blocks of wood glued to the neck to form the heel and angle of the peg head should be from the same piece of wood as the neck. The heel should have a gradual taper from the full neck width down to ¾ of an inch at the lower edge. After the heel has been tapered, a concave made in the sides of the heel make a neater-looking job than just a straight taper. See Figs. 8-5 and 8-6. I shape this concave portion of the heel on the end of a sander. This can be done with hand tools.

The neck must be planned so that the twelfth fret on the fingerboard is directly over the slots cut in the neck for the sides.

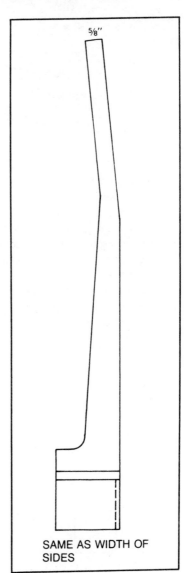

Fig. 8-4. The side view of a guitar neck.

Fig. 8-5. The heel.

After the heel has been shaped, cut the slots in each side of the heel for the side pieces. Clamp a block of wood to the heel and cut the slots with a saw or chisel.

On the mandolin neck, these neck grooves are cut in at an angle. On the guitar, they are cut straight into the neck. Or you can cut at the same angle as the sides are made.

A portion of the neck must be cut away to allow the top of the guitar to be even with the top of the neck. There is *no* tilt between the guitar neck and body as in the mandolin. The body and neck are flat and straight on top.

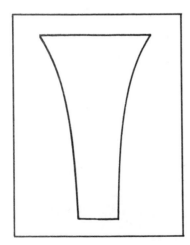

Fig. 8-6. The concave of the guitar heel.

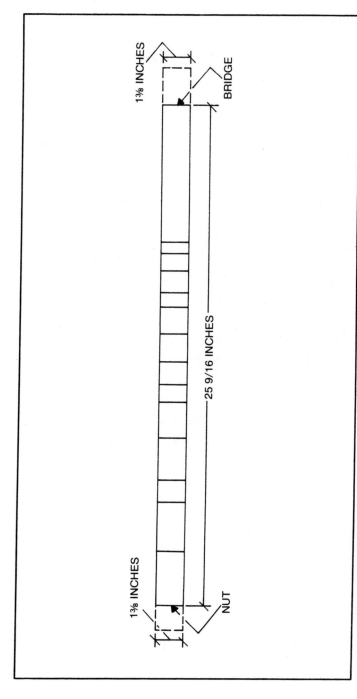

Fig. 8-7. The shape of the guitar sides used in making a form.

## THE SIDES

The sides on the guitar shown in Fig. 2-12 were made from ⅛-inch plywood. One of the most difficult parts of making a guitar is bending the sides. The wood must be heated to a temperature at which the wood will bend. This is not an easy task. There are electrically heated bending forms on the market. One such form can be purchased from the A.E. Overholtzer Company, 618 Orient Street, Chico, CA 95926.

In *The Electric Guitar*, Donald Bresnac writes about using a heated cast-iron pipe to heat the wood. He holds the pipe in a vise and heats the pipe with a propane torch.

Regardless of what kind of wood you use for the sides, or the method you use to make the wood pliable, a form made in the shape of the guitar sides is essential. Make the form to the shape and size given in Fig. 8-7. The side pieces should be about 3½ inches wide. The ends should be cut to fit the neck before bending. The other ends of the side pieces should be cut to length and squared. A stop at one end of the form to butt the end of the side pieces against is essential. This stop is necessary to make sure both side pieces are the same.

The form should be as thick as the sides are wide. Plywood sides can be soaked and bent around the form. Sides made from plywood do not need to be heated before bending. Sides from solid wood can be made by following the instructions in Chapter 10 (see the section on the flat top).

I have never tried to soak and bend the sides made from solid wood. I do not think it will work. Some other method must be used. Regardless of what kind of wood you use for the sides, the side pieces should be left in the form while the lining is glued on. Otherwise, the side pieces will not hold their shape. Two pieces of plywood, ½ inch wide, should be glued to each edge of each side piece for lining. Or the sides can be lined with small blocks of wood. These blocks of wood should be about ⅜ of an inch square and they can be held in place for gluing with spring-type clothespins.

The lining is necessary for gluing space for the top and back. See Fig. 6-6.

## THE END BLOCK

The end block should be ½ by 3½ inches and as long as the sides are wide. The end block will be shaped to fit the curvature of the sides. Spread glue on the end block and clamp until the glue sets.

Before gluing the sides to the neck, make two blocks of wood to fit on each side of the neck and against the sides. See Fig. 3-13. These blocks of wood should be at least an inch square. These blocks glued to the sides and neck make a strong joint. When the sides and neck have been glued, glue in these blocks.

The sides and end block should be glued together on a flat table or workboard. This is necessary to keep the pieces straight and even.

## GLUING THE SIDES TO THE NECK

Refer to Chapter 3 for instructions on gluing the neck and sides together. Fig. 3-12 shows the mandolin neck and sides being glued together.

Pencil a line on the gluing board to make sure the sides are in line with the neck. Mark the center of each end of the neck. Match these marks with the pencil line on the gluing board and clamp the neck in place on the board. The joint where the two sidepieces are glued at the end block should be held on the center line.

A piece of wood as thick as the top, placed between the side pieces and the gluing board, is necessary. Also, a piece of wood the same thickness must be used between the sides at the end block and the gluing board.

It will be best if you use these pieces of wood at intervals of 3 to 4 inches apart, all around the sides, while gluing the neck to the sides. Use waxed paper to keep the unit from becoming glued to the table. The reason for putting wood under the side pieces is to keep the sides straight with the neck.

## THE TOP

Follow the instructions given in Chapter 10. What kind of wood makes a good guitar top? Plywood will not make the best guitar top. If you cannot find other wood, or you are unable to make your own top for any reason, you can make a top for your guitar from plywood. Plywood used for a top must be sanded much thinner than ⅛ of an inch.

Most inexpensive guitars you see in stores have plywood tops. A guitar top made from plywood will not need as much bracing as a top made from solid wood.

Some people say that instrument tops made from spruce produce the best sound. The top on the guitar shown in Fig. 2-12 was made from sitka spruce. It made an excellent top. To make this top, I glued two pieces of sitka spruce together (as in Fig. 10-3) and

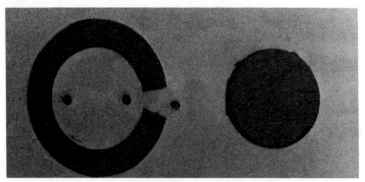

Fig. 8-8. A template to cut the rosette groove and sound hole.

sanded it completely with a vibrator sander. This top is 3/32 of an inch thick.

The top should be made from vertical-grained wood. A guitar top made from vertical-grained wood will be more beautiful. It will be stronger and it will vibrate better than a top made from ordinary wood.

How thick should a top be? It depends on the wood and your ability to work it down (to keep it from breaking and cracking). I kept my top between two plywood door cutouts when I am not working with it. Some people make tops as thin as 1/16 of an inch. Do not try to use a top thicker than ⅛ of an inch. Make it thinner than ⅛ of an inch if you can.

Some people say that nylon strings on a guitar do not put as much pressure on the top as do steel strings. Whether this is true or not I do not know. And I have no way of testing such a theory. The top for a guitar, with nylon strings, can be made thinner than if you were using steel strings.

If you are making your first guitar, you should make the top between 3/32 of an inch and ⅛ of an inch thick.

## THE ROSETTE

Figure 8-8 shows a template for cutting the groove for the rosette and the sound hole. Figure 8-9 shows the router with a template bushing guide installed. The guide follows the contour of the template and holds the router bit the proper distance from the template. A template can be made from ⅜-inch plywood or Masonite.

The rosette groove should be cut before the sound hole is cut out. The template and top can be fastened securely to the workboard with wood screws while cutting the groove. This will keep the template and top from slipping. Use the wood screws where the fingerboard will cover the screw holes.

The other end of the template is fastened the same way to the top and workboard to cut the sound hole. The sound hole can be cut with the router or it can be cut with a knife.

There should be at least one-quarter inch of wood between the sound hole and the rosette. Glue the rosette in the groove and weight it down while the glue dries.

## THE BRACING

One of the problems in making a guitar is bracing the top so that it will remain perfectly flat. The bracing must be light enough so that the top will have good vibration and yet remain flat. A guitar with the bridge glued on the top will vibrate better than a guitar with a tailpiece and floating bridge. The floating bridge is always pushed down by the tension of the strings.

The bridge glued to the top has a tendency to be under a twisting pressure. The front edge of the bridge presses down and the back edge pulls up. Therefore, the guitar top must have bracing underneath to withstand this twisting action.

The top of the guitar shown in Fig. 2-12 was braced with a combination A and X bracing. The bracing in that guitar is ¼ × ⅜ of an inch. There is also ¼-inch thick pieces of wood under the bridge for the string pins to set into. A strip of ⅛-inch plywood was glued over the joint in the top for reinforcement.

The thickness of the top and the size of the bracing must more or less be determined by "feel." By feel, I do not mean the touch of

Fig. 8-9. A router with a template bushing guide.

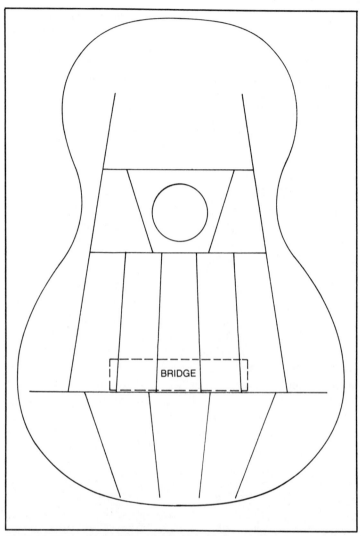

Fig. 8-10. One way to brace a guitar top.

your hand. I mean the sense one has when something is right or wrong.

The top around the sound hole should be left thicker than the rest of the top area. I had a mandolin top that buckled around the sound hole because the wood had been sanded too thin.

If you do make the top the same thickness around the sound hole, brace it well in that area. The thickness of the top and the size of the bracing will be largely determined by the wood you have to use. There are several ways to brace a guitar top. One way is shown in Fig. 8-10.

## THE BACK

Make the back of the guitar the same way as the top. The back of the guitar I used for these plans was made from Philippine mahogany. It was made 3/32 of an inch thick.

Three pieces of ½-×-⅜-inch bracing were glued to the back. The back bracing was also glued to the sides. When I lined the back edge of the sides, I left a space for the bracing to reach the sides. The three pieces of bracing on the back should be evenly spaced between the end of the neck and the end block.

Some people use rubber bands to hold the guitar top and back in place while gluing. I prefer to use weights. To use rubber bands, the top or back must be cut to the exact shape of the sides. It cannot be wider than the sides. If not cut to the exact shape, the downward pull from the rubber bands will split the wood. In using weights, the top/back can be trimmed with a router. When using weights, a perfectly flat board under the guitar and under the weights is necessary.

## THE FINGERBOARD

The fingerboard for my guitar was made from walnut. The fingerboard pattern and fret spacing is given in Fig. 8-11. The string length from nut to bridge for this fret spacing is 25¼ inches. The fingerboard should be made at least one-quarter inch thick.

Instructions are given in Chapter 3 for cutting the kerfs for the frets, installing the frets, and filing the ends. The frets must all be the same height.

When plucked, the strings vibrate. When the strings at the nut and bridge are low enough to make playing the guitar easy, the strings have a tendency to hit the frets when plucked. Much of this can be eliminated by making the fingerboard thinner between the fourth and twelfth frets.

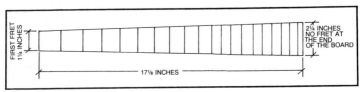

Fig. 8-11. The pattern for a fingerboard.

The fingerboard should be about .010 to .020 thinner between frets 4 and 12. The fingerboard should be made thinner between these frets before the kerfs are cut.

Mother-of-pearl position marks can be inlaid between frets 4 and 5, 7 and 9, and 11 and 12. Position markers are helpful to the player. Any other inlay done on the fingerboard will be for decoration.

Additional small pearl position markers can be inlaid in the edge of the fingerboard next to the players body. When playing the guitar, the player can see the position markers on the edge of the fingerboard easier than those on the face. Holes are drilled for these with a drill press.

To cut out for the fingerboard inlay, hold the inlay in its proper position and tape around the inlay. A steady hand can cut out part of the center portion with a router. Hold a straight piece of hard material on the tape along the edge to run a knife against, and finish cutting with the knife.

I use contact cement to glue the inlay. Glue the fingerboard in place. The fingerboard should be glued in place so that the twelfth fret is situated over the neck and body joint.

## THE PEG HEAD

The head should be ⅝ of an inch thick and 3 inches wide. A pattern for shaping the head is given in Fig. 8-12. A template is necessary for drilling the holes for the keys. The template should be ¾ of an inch thick and 3 inches wide. I use a ¼-inch wood bit to drill the holes. Some keys fit too tight in this ¼-inch hole. When they do, I ream the hole with a 9/32-inch steel bit.

I have trouble finding bushing for the keys. If you can find the bushings, the hole sizes given above will not be applicable. You will need to drill the proper-size hole for the bushing. This hole can only be drilled part way through the head as deep as needed for the bushing. Then it is drill completely through the head with a bit the proper size for the peg.

You will find that some keys or machine heads will have rivets that keep the plate from coming in contact with the wood. You must chip some of the wood away with a small chisel to allow the rivets to be inbedded in the wood.

If you use decorative inlay on the fingerboard, you will also want to use it on the head. I used individual machine heads on the guitar shown in Fig. 2-12. When drilling for individual machine heads, a template is necessary.

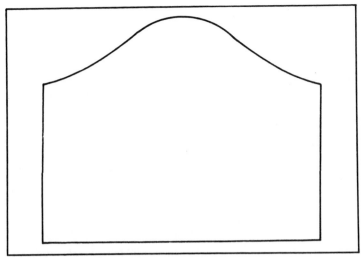

Fig. 8-12. A pattern to shape the peg head end.

A cover must be made to cover the nut on the neck rod. This cover can be made from any material you think suitable. It should be fastened to the wood with small wood screws.

## THE NUT

You can buy a nut from the local music store when you begin to make the guitar. Nuts come in different lengths. If you buy the nut, you can make the fingerboard the same width as the nut is long. A handmade nut should be ¼ of an inch thick and should slope downward toward the head.

The two outside strings should be set in ⅛ of an inch from the edge of the fingerboard. The remainder of the distance between the two outside strings should be divided equally for the other four strings. Cut the notches for the strings just deep enough to accommodate the strings.

## THE BRIDGE

The bridge on the guitar shown in Fig. 2-12 was made from walnut. The saddle was purchased from a music store. The saddle can be removed. The saddle can be filed down to lower the strings or the strings can be raised by putting thin shims under the saddle.

I cut the groove for the saddle on the table saw with a saw blade the same thickness as the saddle. Then I glued a piece of wood in the portion of the saw cut not needed for the saddle. To square off the rounded end of the saw cut, I clamped blocks of wood along the groove and used a drill and knife.

This bridge is 1½ inches wide and 7½ inches long. The portion of the bridge where the saddle is located is ⅜ of an inch high, 5 inches long, and ½ inch wide. A diagram of this bridge is shown in Fig. 8-13. The arms of the bridge and the portion where the string pins are located was worked down to less than ¼ of an inch. Figure 8-14 shows the bridge on the guitar.

The string pins are tapered. To drill these holes, I took a 13/64-size bit and inserted the bit in a drill. With the drill turning, I ground the bit to proper size and taper on the electric grinder.

There are different styles of guitar bridges that you can make. Figure 6-7 shows the string holes being drilled in a bridge. On this style bridge, the holes are drilled through the edge of the bridge. A piece of fret wire is used for the saddle. If you use string pins, the wood on each side of the saddle should be one-quarter inch. The remaining part of the wood is cut down until the bridge is about 3/16 of an inch thick on the back edge. The arms of the bridge should be sloped and thinned down the same way.

Chapter 6 explains how to use dowel pins when gluing the bridge to the top. Sometimes a bridge will pull loose from the tension of the strings.

A C-clamp can be used through the sound hole when you are gluing the bridge to the instrument. The bridge can be held by hand while the glue sets. It also can be held by light weights.

## STRING HEIGHT

The nut and the bridge saddle must be made the correct height so that the strings clear the first fret. At the twelfth fret, the strings should clear the fret by ⅛ of an inch. If the strings vibrate against the

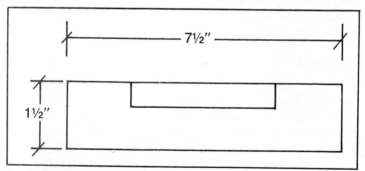

Fig. 8-13. A diagram of the guitar bridge.

Fig. 8-14. The bridge glued on the guitar.

frets, when plucked open at this height, the bridge saddle must be raised. You will need to make a new nut (which would be slightly higher).

## THE PICK GUARD

Guitar tops can be damaged by the pick. I saw (on television) a guitar with a large hole in the top made from the pick. The player must have used a steel pick on that guitar to do so much damage.

Before the rosette is glued in the top, you should trace around one side of the rosette on paper. Save the paper and use it to cut the pick guard and fit it neatly against the rosette.

The pick guard should be glued to the top with contact cement. Mask it off before finishing the guitar.

The guitar shown in Fig. 2-12 was sprayed with a lacquer finish. Refer to Chapter 12 and the section on finishing instruments.

# Chapter 9

# Violin

There is a greater challenge in making the violin than any other instrument described in this book. The violin is really a carved instrument. If you are a wood carver, then the making of a violin will not be such a great challenge. Anyone can carve out the parts of a violin and glue them together to make an instrument. It just takes patience and determination.

It is not known when or where the violin was invented or whether there was a gradual development of the instrument. History seems to indicate that the violin was perfect as it was first made. Some people believe that better violins cannot be made than those created by the masters Stradivari, Amati, Stainer, and others. This should not prevent people like you and me from making violins or even hoping to make better ones than the old masters.

As with other instruments, I used different kinds of wood in making the violin shown in Fig. 2-13. The neck was made from walnut. The top was made from Philippine mahogany. I made the back from two pieces of walnut and one piece from maple. The bridge was made from cherry. The pegs, the end pin and the bow were made from ash. I purchased the fingerboard and tailpiece, which are ebony, and I made the nut from ebony. I am very proud of this violin.

## THE NECK

As with any other stringed instrument, the neck must be made from a hard, close-grained wood. The neck on the violin, shown in

Fig. 2-13, was made from walnut. The piece of wood you select for the neck must be 1¾ inches wide, 2 inches thick, and 11 inches long.

Refer to Fig. 9-1, the front view, and mark the neck. Draw a center line the full length of the neck wood. Use a square and mark a line across the neck 4½ inches from one end. This mark is where the fingerboard begins. This is the starting point.

Mark the neck for the fingerboard. Measure each way from the center line to make sure the fingerboard will be in the center of the wood. The fingerboard will be ⅞ of an inch wide at the narrow end. It will be 1¼ inches wide at the neck and body joint. The neck and body joint will be 5 7/16 inches from the mark where the fingerboard begins. Figure 9-2 shows the side view of the neck.

Refer to Fig. 9-3 and mark the shape of the scroll and peg box. This is an actual-size drawing. As you can see, the top portion of the scroll is slightly higher than the neck line. A piece of wood ¼ inch thick can be glued to the neck wood so that the top of the scroll will be about the same height as the top of the fingerboard. Also, a piece of wood can be glued to the underside of the neck wood to provide thickness for the scroll.

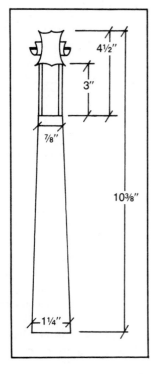

Fig. 9-1. A front view of the violin neck.

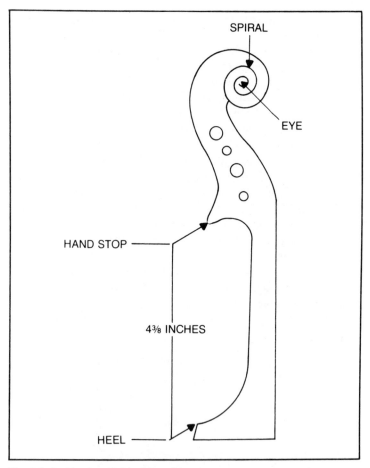

Fig. 9-2. A side view of the violin neck.

You should cut out the round portion of the scroll and the peg box on a band saw after marking. Sand the saw mark down so that the neck center line can be extended around the end of the wood and the back side of the peg box. Mark the center of the scroll and peg box.

Near the peg box, the scroll should be ⅞ of an inch wide. A gradual taper should be marked so the scroll will be ⅜ of an inch wide, half the distance around the scroll.

The taper as it comes back to the lower edge of the peg box should be ⅞ of an inch. The eye of the scroll should be centered ¾ of an inch from the top edge of the wood.

Now you are ready to begin carving the scroll.

## THE SCROLL

The scroll should be carved before the neck is shaped. This allows you to clamp the neck to a work bench while the carving is done. Begin carving around the eye. The spiral should begin right from the lower edge of the eye and on the side of the eye toward the instrument. As you work at carving the scroll, you will get insight into how it should be done.

Do not attempt to cut away large chips of wood at a time. Take your time and make little chips. Do not attempt to carve the scroll to the finished dimensions. Leave a little wood outside the marks to sand down to the size given above. Work at it until it suits you; your scroll need not look exactly like someone else's scroll.

Be careful that the wood does not splinter or chip along the edge of the spiral. This edge is thin and it chips easily.

## THE PEG BOX

The peg box is the part of the neck between the scroll and the fingerboard. See Fig. 9-4. The peg box is hollowed out of the solid wood. The tuning pegs pass through the sides of the peg box and the strings are wound around the pegs within the box. You should hollow out only as much wood as is necessary. Leave the sides of the box strong.

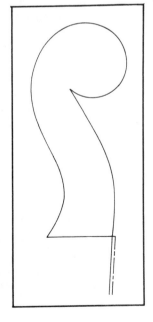

Fig. 9-3. The scroll and the peg box.

Fig. 9-4. The peg box.

The outside width of the peg box is ⅞ of an inch. You should leave a strong ⅛ of an inch of wood to form the sides of the box at the top edge. As the box is hollowed out, gradually slope the sides inward so the box is narrower at the bottom than at the top. Make the box only as deep as necessary to allow room for the strings to wind around the pegs. The peg box should begin ¼ of an inch from the end of the fingerboard position and extend to the scroll. The nut will fit on this ¼-inch piece of wood.

The peg holes must be tapered. A reamer designed especially to ream the holes can be purchased.

I made the peg holes for the violin, shown in Fig. 2-13, by drilling a ¼-inch hole through both sides of the peg box. Then the holes were reamed with a round, rat-tailed wood rasp. The pegs were then made to fit the holes.

You will find a pattern for the peg holes shown in Fig. 9-5. When tapering the peg holes, be sure two holes are tapered from each side of the peg box.

The violin shown in Fig. 2-13 is a left-hand violin. The position of the tuning pegs makes a violin either a right-hand or a left-hand instrument. To play this instrument in the right-hand position, the tuning peg nearest the nut will crowd the hand. This makes fingering the strings at the end of the fingerboard difficult. At the time these pictures were taken, the strings were on the instrument in the normal playing position. Make sure when you ream the holes for the tuning pegs that the position of the pegs will be reversed from those in the photograph (unless you are making a left-hand violin).

A double scallop should be made on the outside portion of the scroll and the underside of the peg box. Use a center line on this part of the wood and, with hand tools, work out a groove or a scallop on each side of the line. See Fig. 9-6.

## SHAPING THE NECK

The scroll and peg box are the difficult parts of the neck to make. Shaping the rest of the neck is easy. The distance from the handstop to the front edge of the heel, shown in Fig. 9-2, is 4⅜ inches.

If you buy the fingerboard, you must make the neck width to fit the fingerboard. You can make a fingerboard. The dimensions of the fingerboard are ⅞ of an inch at the narrow end, 1¼ inches where the neck joins the body, and it is 10½ to 11¼ inches long.

The fingerboard for the violin cannot be made flat. It must be arched. A bow cannot be used on a flat fingerboard. Besides being arched, the fingerboard should be higher above the violin top on the G string side than it is on the other side by about 3/32 of an inch. This facilitates the use of the bow.

To make the fingerboard higher on one side than the other, the top of the neck—where the fingerboard will be glued—can be beveled. This bevel can be made by hand or a tapered piece of wood can be held on the jointer table (raising one side of the neck) and the neck can be beveled on a jointer.

The fingerboard does not rest flat on the top of the violin. There is space between the fingerboard and the top. See Fig. 9-7.

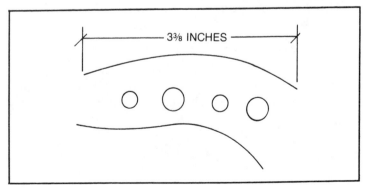

3⅜ INCHES

Fig. 9-5. The peg hole pattern.

Fig. 9-6. The scallop around the scroll and the back of the peg box.

Because of the curvature of the violin top, the neck and body must be glued together just right to allow the fingerboard to reach over the top to clear the curvature.

## BENDING THE SIDES

The sides of the violin are usually called ribs. For continuity of thought, I refer to them in this book as sides. With one exception, the sides are built by using the same procedure as the sides for the plucked dulcimer described in Chapter 5. In Chapter 5, there are instructions for building both sides of the instrument at the same time. Violin sides should be built one side at a time.

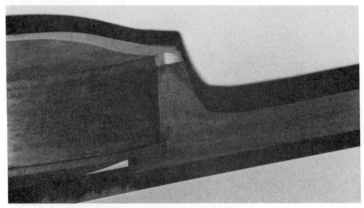

Fig. 9-7. The neck and the body joint.

The shape of one side of the violin is shown in Fig. 9-8. Lay off the shape of the violin on a workboard and cover the board with waxed paper. Each violin side is made up of three pieces. Refer to Fig. 9-8 and make a form for each side piece.

The side pieces should be 1 3/16 inches wide. Cut the side pieces long enough to reach around the form with wood to spare for trimming the ends. Cut the sides as thin as necessary (about 1/16 of an inch), but leave them as thick as possible—to bend around the form.

Boil, soak, or heat the wood to make it pliable for bending. Bend the side pieces around the form and hold it with clamps or rubber bands while the wood dries to shape. I cut the side piece about 1/16 of an inch thick and boiled the pieces in water. This worked for me.

## THE CORNER BLOCKS

The corner blocks should be made from the same piece of wood as the sides. The corner blocks will be more or less V shaped. You can let the pointed portion of the corner block form the actual corner of the instrument or the side pieces can be glued together to make the corners (with the corner blocks made to fit inside to give support).

Clamp the corner blocks to the workboard and glue the side pieces to the corner blocks. While the glued side pieces are still on the workboard, a ⅛-inch piece of plywood should be glued to the inside of the side pieces to make enough gluing surface for the top and back. Or small pieces of wood can be glued to the edges of the sides to make the gluing surface.

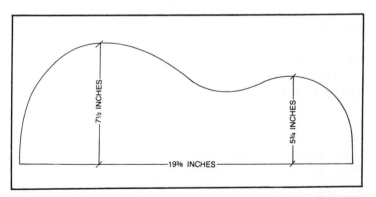

Fig. 9-8. A pattern of one-half of the violin used in making a form to bend the sides.

Fig. 9-9. The dovetail block.

Remove this side piece unit from the workboard and make the other unit the same way. The two side pieces should be exactly alike.

## THE END BLOCK

An end block made from ½-×-1 3/16-×-2-inch hardwood is used to hold the ends of the side pieces and glue the side piece to the end block.

## THE DOVETAIL BLOCK

A tapered dovetail block (as in Fig. 9-9) should be made for the neck to be glued into. The side pieces at the neck end are glued to the dovetail block before the neck is glued into the block.

Care must be taken in making the dovetail block. The heel of the neck must fit perfectly in this block. The corners of the block must be rounded to fit the ends of the side pieces. The inside corners of the block should also be rounded. The width of the heel must be right so that the fingerboard will clear the body of the violin. The end of the neck must be cut off at an angle to cause the fingerboard to clear the curvature of the violin top (see Fig. 9-7).

The neck can be cut at an angle on a radial arm saw. A block of wood the proper thickness must be used under the end of the neck to raise the end the proper distance off the table to cut the neck at an angle. You are now ready to glue the side pieces to the dovetail block and the neck into the block.

## THE TOP

Make the top according to the instructions given in Chapter 10.

Fig. 9-10. A cross section of a violin top (side to side).

Figure 9-10 shows a cross section as if it were cut from side to side. Figure 9-11 is a view of the top if it were cut in half from the end block to the neck.

A notch must be cut in the top to fit neatly around the neck. Also, a notch must be cut in the opposite end of the top directly over the end block. This notch should be cut ¼ of an inch into the top, and 1¼ inches long. A piece of hardwood must be made to fit and be glued in this space. The purpose of this piece of wood is to prevent the string that holds the tailpiece from splitting the top. This is a saddle and should be at least 3/16 of an inch higher than the top of the instrument. The part above the top should be shaped like an upside down V or a very blunt wedge. Glue the neck in the dovetail joint. Glue the top to the sides.

## THE F HOLES

Refer to Fig. 9-12 and drill properly spaced holes to start cutting the sound holes. Cut the F holes with a knife or small saw blade. You can judge the thickness of the top through the sound holes. The top should be about ⅛ of an inch thick. Sand the top thinner than ⅛ of an inch near the side pieces. This will cause better vibration of the top and the violin will sound better.

After the fingerboard has been glued in position, make a small notch in each F hole. These notches are made on the inside edge of the F hole. These notches are to mark the bridge location. The measurement for the bridge position is 13⅛ inches from the narrow end of the fingerboard.

## THE BASS BAR

There is no inside bracing in a violin top. The bass bar is ⅛ of an inch thick, ¼ of an inch wide and 7¾ inches long.

Fig. 9-11. A cross section of a violin top (end to end).

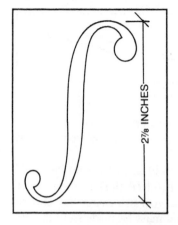

Fig. 9-12. An F hole pattern.

2⅞ INCHES

Mark the exact center of the underside of the top. The center of the bass bar will be located at the notched bridge position. It will be glued in place one-half inch over from the center line at the notches (toward the bass string side of the top). Position the bass bar in such a way that the end nearest the neck is ⅛ of an inch closer to the center line than it is at the center near the notches in the F hole. Glue the bass bar and allow the glue to set. Figure 9-13 shows the bass bar.

## THE BACK

The back should be made from a hard wood. Maple is commonly used. Nevertheless, any hard wood should make a good violin back. Follow the instructions given in Chapter 10 to make the back.

Before gluing the back to the instrument, be sure to measure the length of the sound post. Hold a straightedge across the sides at

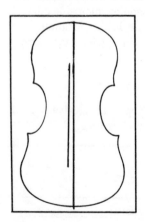

Fig. 9-13. The bass bar.

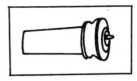

Fig. 9-14. The end pin.

the sound post position and measure from the straightedge to the inside of the top. You must also measure the depth of the arch in the back. Add the two measurements and you will have the length of the sound post.

Glue the fingerboard in place. Make the nut out of hardwood and glue it in place. The top portion of the nut should slope slightly toward the peg box. The nut must be higher than the fingerboard to offer string clearance.

Notches must be cut in the nut for the strings. Be sure the strings do not touch the end of the fingerboard.

## THE END PIN

Drill a one-quarter inch hole through the end block. This hole is for the end pin. The tailpiece is fastened to the end pin by means of a string that you purchase along with the tailpiece. The hole for the end pin must be in line with the center of the fingerboard. Taper this hole and make a pin out of hardwood to fit the hole. Shape the pin so that it looks neat. See Fig. 9-14.

## THE BRIDGE

A pattern for the bridge is given in Fig. 9-15. The feet of the bridge should be one-quarter inch wide. The bridge should be thinner at the top like a wedge. You will determine the bridge height after attaching the tailpiece and strings. The bridge must be made from hardwood.

Fig. 9-15. The violin bridge.

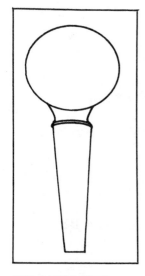

Fig. 9-16. A peg.

## THE SOUND POST

The sound post is crucial to the sound of the violin. The positioning of the post a fraction of an inch forward or backward, right or left, will alter the sound of the instrument.

The sound post should be about ¼ of an inch in diameter. A ¼-inch dowel will make a good sound post. The recommended position for the post is ⅛ of an inch behind the right foot of the bridge and centered between the first and second strings.

The inside of arched instruments should be smooth and well sanded. This is especially important for that portion where the sound post will be positioned.

If it is not sanded smooth, the setting of the sound post will be very difficult. After the top has been glued to the sides, the position of the sound post should be estimated.

Measure the length of the sound post before gluing the back on the violin. Study Chapter 12 on final sanding and finishing of an instrument. The violin shown in Fig. 2-13 was finished with Truoil.

## THE PEGS

The tuning pegs must be made from hardwood. The strings will cut into softwood. The stem part of the pegs should be made on a lathe. Then taper the pegs down by hand until they fit the peg holes. Each peg hole may have its own pin.

Figure 9-16 shows a tuning peg. After shaping the round outside portion of the peg heads, a scallop should be sanded into the sides of each peg head. Work down the edge of a board until it is rounded like the scallop should be. Glue sandpaper to the edge of the board to make a sanding block. I find this an easy way to sand the scallop out of the sides of the peg heads.

## THE BOW

The bow should be made from perfectly straight-grained wood. This is difficult to find. If you know someone who splits out wood for axle handles who would let you have some wood for a bow, this would be great.

The wood for the bow should be tough. The bow shown in Fig. 2-13 was made from ash.

The piece of wood for the bow should be one-half inch thick and 1 inch wide. It must be 28½ inches long. The bow, when completed, should be ⅜ of an inch in diameter at the frog end and tapered to ¼ of an inch or less at the tip end.

One edge of the piece of wood should be sanded smooth. Draw a center line on this edge from end to end. In the end of the wood where the frog will be located, drill a hole for the frog screw. This hole should be drilled with a ⅛-inch bit. Check the size of the frog screw for the proper bit size.

Drill at least 1¼ inches into the end of the wood. The hole for the frog screw must be centered in the wood so that you can work the wood to ⅜ of an inch when completed.

The tip of the bow should be shaped as in Fig. 9-17. The tip should be ¾ of an inch high from the back of the bow and tapered wide to at least ⅜ of an inch at the top (or face) of the tip.

Much of the excess wood can be cut off on the band saw. You should use your center line on the back side of the wood to keep it straight. After the bow is completed, it should be curved slightly backward. This is done by making a bending board (as in Fig. 9-18).

Steam the bow and clamp it to the board in such a manner that the bow will remain straight one way and be bent backward. It took

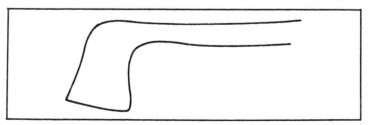

Fig. 9-17. The bow tip.

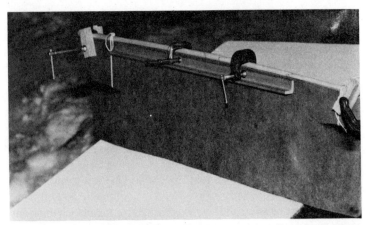

Fig. 9-18. A bow bending board.

me three turns of steaming and bending to get the proper bend on the bow shown in Fig. 2-13.

The notch for the frog should begin ¾ of an inch from the end of the bow. The notch should be ¾ of an inch long and wide enough to accommodate the frog screw nut. See Fig. 9-19. The notch can be cut out with a knife. After the frog notch is completed, drill a smaller hole (an extension of the ⅛-inch hole) into the bow for the smaller end of the frog screw.

A small square hole must be carved in the tip for the bow hair. See Fig. 9-20. This hole is tapered toward the bottom.

## THE BOW HAIR-TIP END

The bow hair is not glued into the socket; it is held with a small wedge. Tie one end of the hair near the end. Place the end of the bow hair into the socket in the bow tip. Make a wedge. Press the wedge firmly in the socket against the hair. Use the wedge on the side of the hair so that when the hair is in the frog it will cover the wedge.

You will have to use the trial-and-error method in making the proper size and shape wedge. When you get it right, the wedge will hold the hair in the tip securely.

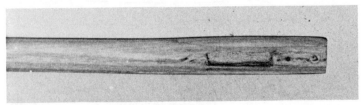

Fig. 9-19. The notch in the bow for the frog.

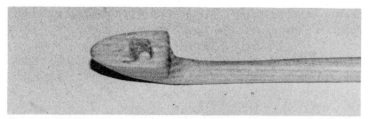

Fig. 9-20. Note the hole in the tip of the box for the bow hair.

## THE FROG END

Place the frog in the notch in the bow without the screw. Just hold it there. The frog must be properly positioned so that the hair will tighten and loosen. The nut for the screw should be ¼ of an inch from the front end of the notch. Mark this frog position with tape on the bow.

Remove the ferrule from the front end of the frog. There is a strip of plastic, called a *bow slide*, that must be removed to attach the hair to the frog. Pull the bow slide forward out of the frog. Do not lift up; it will break. See Fig. 9-21.

The hair socket has been made in the frog. The bow hair will be secured in the socket with a small wedge. Comb the bow hair. Measure the hair and cut it to length. Slip the ferrule over the bow hair. Wedge the hair in the socket. Replace the bow slide and ferrule. If the hair is loose inside the ferrule, you will need to use a small piece of wood between the hair and the ferrule so that it will have a snug fit. Fasten the frog in the notch with the screw. Use the same kind of finish on the bow as you use on the violin.

The stem part of the tuning pegs must be masked off so that no finish material gets on the stems. They will not stay tight in the

Fig. 9-21. A dismantled frog.

holes if finish material is on them. The peg holes must be plugged to keep the finish out of the holes.

Drill a small hole in each peg stem for the strings to be passed through before winding the strings around the pegs. If necessary, you can scrape some bow rosin off and rub it on the peg stems to make them stick and hold in the holes.

You are now ready to "string up" your violin. The smallest string—the one nearest the bow—will be tuned to E pitch (the E higher than middle C). The next string is tuned to A (the A above middle C). The third string is tuned to D and the fourth string is tuned to G (the G note below middle C on the piano).

As I was making the violin shown in Fig. 2-13, I had the feeling that it would be a good-sounding instrument. I expected it to have a good tone. Because I am not a trained musician, I could not test it myself. So I took it to a professional violinist to have it played. I expected an honest report. If he had anything good to say about the violin, he would say it—perhaps grudgingly. The violin sounded better than I expected. The violinist spoke highly of the tonal qualities and sound of the instrument. This gave me much pleasure.

# Chapter 10

# Instrument Tops from Solid Wood

Imagine walking in the snow on a cold morning. The snow snaps and crunches under your feet. Later the same day, you can walk the same path, but the sound of your walking in the snow will be different. It will be more soft and mellow as the temperature rises and the snow softens. The sound of your instrument depends largely on the kind of wood you use for the top.

## AVAILABILITY OF WOOD

A hard wood, whether it is plywood or a solid, close-grained wood, will produce a sharp, crisp, clear tone. A soft wood seems to absorb some of the vibrations rather than transmitting them, and it will produce a soft, mellow tone. Who can say which is the best tone? It is really a matter of preference.

You must consider several factors when you are deciding what kind of wood to use for the top of an instrument. You must consider:

☐ The sound you want from your instrument (sharp and crisp or soft and mellow).

☐ The tools you have to work with.

☐ The possibility that some wood will be ruined in the process of making a top.

You might have a piece of wood about ready to glue to an instrument when it splits or warps. This sometimes happens to all craftsmen. It can be very disappointing and frustrating.

## BEAUTY MUST BE CONSIDERED

Choose wood wisely. It should be a close-grained wood and free of knots. The top on the mandolin shown in Fig. 2-2 was made

115

from sumac. Sumac is a bush. It grows fast and it has a short life span. The wood is coarse grained and the grain has a tendency to be pithy.

Because it is pithy, sumac alone would not make a good instrument top. It would break apart. Therefore, I glued the sumac to a piece of thin veneer and sanded both sides to get the required thickness. Why did I use sumac, a pithy wood, for a top? Because it is a beautiful wood. Its colors are green, yellow, white, and brown. The sumac has nothing to do with the sound of the mandolin. The veneer backing gives it a sharp, crisp tone.

Figure 2-3 shows a mandolin made from Philippine mahogany; the neck and bridge were made from walnut. This mahogany is a beautiful wood and the mandolin has a good sound.

The method of making an instrument from solid wood is the same as using plywood—except on two points. Straight-grained wood must have cross bracing glued to the underside of the top. This is in addition to the inside bracing. Instrument sides made from plywood can be soaked in water and bent to shape. Sides made from solid wood cannot be bent as easily. The sides of the mandolin shown in Fig. 2-3 were made from mahogany, a solid wood.

It was necessary for me to boil the wood from which the sides were made. Different methods are used in the bending of wood. Donald Brosnac, in his book *The Electric Guitar*, mentions that he uses a cast-iron pipe heated with a propane torch to heat the wood and make it pliable for bending.

The wood you select for the instrument top must be straight. It is difficult to work with wood that is curved or warped like a rainbow.

### THE FLAT TOP

Instrument sides and tops can be made from wood of almost any size. For the following instructions, use a board ¾ × 6 inches. It should be at least 6 inches longer than needed for the top. This allows some extra wood for a margin of error.

This board will make two pieces of wood. That is enough for one instrument top.

### SANDING, GLUING, AND JOINTING

The ¾-inch board must first be sanded or planed (if it is not already smooth). After sanding, both edges should be run over a jointer. See Fig. 10-1. The edges must be free of chipped places. A chipped place on the edge of the board will result in a defect in the top.

Fig. 10-1. Smoothing the edge of a board on the jointer.

The board must be ripped on a band saw to make two pieces of wood for the top. Refer to Fig. 10-2. The fence or guide on the band saw should be set ⅜ of an inch from the blade. The fence must stand square with the blade so that both pieces will be uniform. Both pieces should be about the same thickness on the edges and all the way through—not thick and thin.

The two thin pieces of wood you have cut must be glued together to make a top. Figure 10-3 shows two pieces of wood being glued together. The two thin pieces of wood should be carefully matched and fitted before gluing. The sanded side of each piece should be turned up. Hold the edges together. Switch ends and match the grain. You want to get the best grain pattern possible. Also, the pieces should be held up toward the light to see how they fit. Do they fit together to provide a good joint?

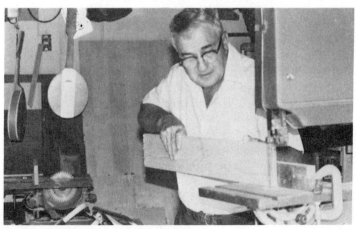
Fig. 10-2. Ripping the board on the band saw.

Fig. 10-3. Gluing the boards to make a top.

When you are satisfied with the fit, glue the two pieces together as in Fig. 10-3. Spread glue on the edges of both pieces of wood. The clamps should not all be on the same side of the board. There should be two on one side at the ends and one in the middle on the other side. It might be necessary to wedge between the clamps and the board; this will help to keep the board straight.

After the glue has set, begin sanding on the smooth side of the board. A vibrator with fine sandpaper should be used. This will be the top side of the wood. It should be thoroughly sanded. If the grain of the wood matched well, with a good sanding job the glue joint might not show. See Fig. 10-4.

## USING DADO HEADS TO SHAVE THE TOP

Dado heads are a number of different kinds of saw blades used

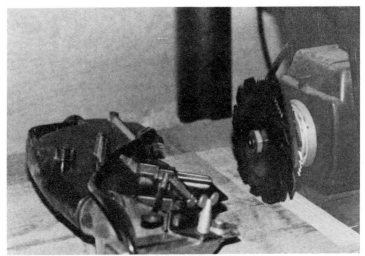

Fig. 10-4. Shaving the top with dado heads.

at the same time. Figure 10-5 shows the dado heads being used on a radial arm saw. The blades are pulled across the wood to shave it away.

The ⅜-inch thick board will soon be shaved down to the required thickness. This wastes a little wood, but it is one way to do the job. The table of the saw must be square with the arm or one edge of the board will be thicker than the other.

Figure 10-5 shows the dado heads without the guard or cover in place. Do not attempt to use dado heads without the blade guard in

Fig. 10-5. Wood for a top (with a belt and vibrator sander).

place. The guard was left off only for the taking of the picture. Do not use tools that are unsafe.

Do not attempt to shave very much wood at a time. The dado heads, when set for a deep cut, have a tendency to walk or jump. Be careful. The top should be shaved to about ⅛ of an inch thickness.

The side of the board not previously sanded must be sanded after the use of the dado heads. You will want to finish sanding with a vibrator using finishing paper. See Fig. 10-4.

Do not leave an unfinished top laying on a table overnight. The top should be hung up or left in a leaning position so that the air will circulate around it.

## CROSS BRACING

Tops made from solid wood must have cross bracing glued to the underside. Thin wood such as ⅛-inch plywood will make acceptable bracing for mandolin or dulcimer tops. A guitar top must have sturdier bracing than plywood because there is no inside bracing in a guitar.

A mandolin top should have one strip of bracing centered between the inside bracing and the end block. Another strip of plywood between the inside bracing and the sound hole should be used. One method of bracing around the sound hole is to cut a 2½-inch diameter hole out of ⅛-inch plywood, 4½ inches square, and glue around the sound hole.

Thin pieces of wood should be glued over the joint where the two top pieces meet. Cross bracing for dulcimer tops should be used between the sound holes.

## THE ARCH TOP

There is more than one way to make arched tops for musical instruments. The method outlined here is one of the easier ways.

### The Outside of the Top

Select a good piece of wood for the top. It must be free of knots and preferably it should be vertical grained. The wood should be at least ¾ of an inch thick. A piece of wood this thick will give you an arch of almost ¾ inches. If you want a higher arch, you will need thicker wood.

Cut the wood square to the largest dimension needed for the top. If it is a violin top you are making, you must add at least ¼ of an inch to these dimensions. A violin top should extend over the sides about ⅛ of an inch.

Mark the shape of the arch on the end of the wood. The violin top should be at least ⅛ of an inch thick when completely sanded, a mandolin top should be 5/16 of an inch thick, and a guitar arched top should be at least ¼ of an inch thick when sanded.

Use a table saw to cut away most of the excess wood. See Fig. 10-6.

Set the fence of the saw ¼ of an inch from the blade. Adjust the blade to cut to the mark. Make a cut along each side of the board. Leave the ¼ inch of wood on each side to hold the board while cutting.

Move the fence over the distances of the thickness of the saw blade. Make a cut along each side of the board. Follow this procedure and keep raising or lowering the saw blade accordingly until you have cut the wood away.

The ends of the arched top can be cut the same way with a table saw or radial arm saw. When cutting the ends of the arch, it is not necessary to leave the ¼ inch of wood on the end as you did the sides.

After the ends of the arch have been cut, the ¼ inch of wood on each side must be cut off. This can be done by adjusting the fence and saw blade. Hold the wood on edge against the fence and cut the ¼ inch of wood off.

Figure 10-7 shows my 6-×-48 sander. I used the end of the sander to sand the outside top/back of the violin after cutting on the table saw. Figure 10-8 shows an assortment of tools. These are the only tools I used in making the violin shown in Fig. 2-13. I do not have an elaborate set of carving knives. You can improvise and accomplish a lot with a little. Your determination and patience is what counts.

Fig. 10-6. Using a table saw to cut away excess wood.

Fig. 10 -7. Using a belt sander to sand away wood from a violin top.

If you do not have a sander that uses a 6-×-48 belt, a hand held belt sander will be useful. If you do not have a belt sander, use knives and carve the top out.

### The Underside of the Top

You should have the outside part of the top well in hand by now. Cut out the top to the shape of the instrument. Use the pattern for

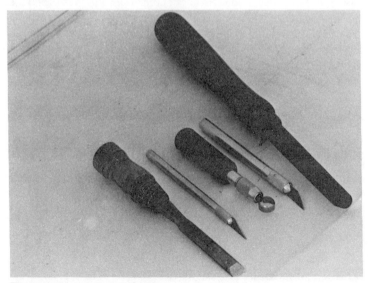

Fig. 10 -8. An assortment of tools.

the F hole shown in Fig. 9-12 and mark the F holes on the outside of the top.

Choose the proper size drill bit and drill holes through the top at the end of the F holes. The reason for drilling the holes at this time is that you can gauge the thickness of the top through the drilled holes.

Much of the excess wood on the underside of the top can be cut away with the table saw. You cannot cut the full length of the wood. You must leave a flat edge to glue the top to the sides. With the power turned on the saw, the piece of wood must be lowered on the whirring saw blade. Then pushed along the table the proper distance. Stop the saw blade and lift the wood up. You must mark the saw table or fence so that you do not cut too far and ruin the top. I use masking tape on the fence to mark where to lower the wood and where to stop cutting.

The round-ended tool (that doesn't look like a knife) shown in Fig. 10-8 is a handy scraper to scrape the excess wood out of the underside of the top. This scraper will soon tear up a piece of wood. This scraper comes with a set of X-Acto tools. All you need to do is scrape and carve the wood away from the underside of the top. It takes work, patience, and determination, but it can be done. The finished instrument will be worth all your hours of toil.

# Chapter 11

# Binding Musical Instruments

Binding, or *purfling* as it is sometimes called, is an edging that is glued around the edge of an instrument. It's use is important to an instrument. Binding protects the edges that might otherwise become chipped or dented. It also adds to the appearance of an instrument. The exposed edge of a piece of wood does not look as nice as the flat surface. Also, binding seals out moisture.

## PLASTIC BINDING

There are different types of binding to select. An ivoroid binding was used on my instruments pictured in this book (except the guitar shown in Fig. 2-12).

Let the beauty of the wood speak for itself rather than adorn the instrument with a lot of unnecessary edging and inlay. My concern is not to make an instrument that looks like it came out of a store, but one that looks handmade.

You can purchase binding from any number of sources. It can be purchased through your local music store or ordered by mail from suppliers listed at the end of this book.

A groove must be cut around the edge of the instrument for the binding. This groove is cut with a router. The router must be fitted with a trimmer attachment. A trimmer attachment is a roller that rolls against the body of the instrument as the router is moved. The roller is set so that the bit cuts the required depth and no more.

Refer to Fig. 11-1 when adjusting the router. The photograph shows a gauge used to adjust the width and depth of the cut. This gauge is merely a block of wood with different width and thickness of the binding glued to the edge of the wood. The gauge is held against the roller while the bit is adjusted.

The router adjustment should be tested on scrap wood before you begin to cut a groove on an instrument. Fig. 11-2 shows the groove being cut.

If you do not have a stand or table for the router or someone to hold the router while you cut the groove, the top and back of an instrument can be left wider than the body and clamps can be used to hold the instrument. Clamp the back to the table and rout the top edge. Then the neck can be clamped to the table to rout the back edge. A dulcimer can be clamped to the table at the end blocks to hold the instrument while routing.

Fig. 11-1. Adjusting the router.

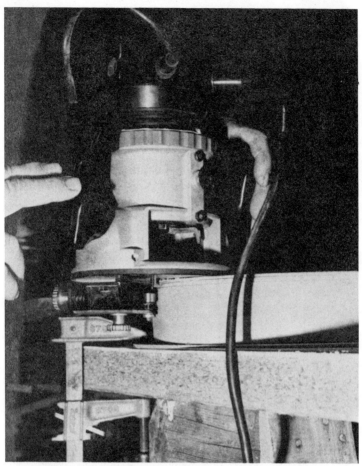

Fig. 11-2. Routing the groove for binding.

To prevent the wood from chipping (especially a top made from solid wood), you should begin with the router at the widest point of the body and work toward the head or neck and the tail or end block.

The groove cannot be completely cut with a router near the neck and heel on the instrument. The ends of the groove must be cut out by hand with a knife.

The binding can also be run all the way around the heel. Much of the groove must be cut by hand. See Fig. 11-3.

The binding I use comes in a length that I can use a full piece on the back of a mandolin and there is enough left out of the strip of binding to go half way around the front. The two pieces of binding on the front are joined under the tailpiece. The long pieces should be held in place while marking the length. A snug fit is important.

The binding must be glued to the back edge before the short pieces can be cut and fitted around the heel of the instrument. The edge of the binding can be scraped with the back edge of a knife. A file can also be used on the edge of the binding to work it down even with the wood.

You should ask your supplier about the kind of glue to use on the binding. If no gluing instructions are given, you can experiment with different kinds of glue. I seem to get along best with contact cement.

## WOOD PURFLING

Some instruments are bound with wood purfling rather than plastic binding. Plastic is easier to use than wood, but wood purfling makes a better-looking instrument.

There are two kinds of wood purfling. You can buy purfling that is all one color, black, or white, etc. There is a purfling you can buy that has a wood design glued up similar to a rosette. That is what I used on the guitar shown in Fig. 2-12. This makes a nice-looking instrument.

Purfling is easy to break. It should be bent around a form the shape as the guitar sides before you attempt to glue it to the

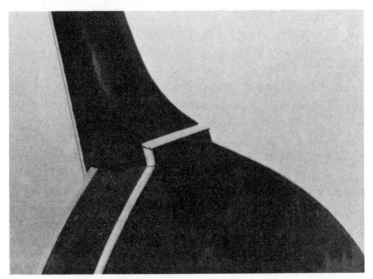

Fig. 11-3. The binding all around the heel.

instrument. If it breaks, you can butt the two ends together. You must be careful to make the joint look as neat as possible.

Two pieces of the solid purfling can be joined by filing a bevel on the ends and overlapping the pieces. Use a glue that is easy to clean up. Excess glue that squeezes out around the edge of the binding should be cleaned up before it dries. Use rubber bands to hold the binding in place while the glue sets. Binding on a guitar or mandolin protects the edge of the wood and seals moisture out.

The purfling on a violin is not glued to the edge of the wood; it is inlaid in the face or flat surface near the edge of the wood. Its purpose is decorative and also it will prevent the wood from splitting. A violin should have purfling around the edges. Purfling has not been attached to the violin shown in Fig. 2-13.

Purfling on a violin is different from the binding on other instruments. A special tool (a purfling cutter) is used to cut the groove for the purfling.

You can use either one-line or two-line purfling. A one-line purfling should be set in about 3/16 of an inch from the edge of the wood. The second of a two-line purfling should be set about 1/16 of an inch inside the first line. The groove for the purfling should be cut about 1/32 of an inch deep. You should not attempt to cut this deep a channel at one time. Make several passes with the cutter around the edge of the instrument.

When using a hand-held purfling cutter or a power router, you should always cut with the grain. That is so the grain of the wood will lead the tool out of the wood. When cutting against the grain, the tool will catch in the grain of the wood and cause the wood to crack or split.

# Chapter 12

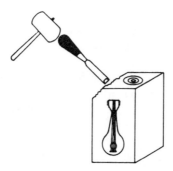

# Sanding, Staining, and Finishing

You must take as much care in finishing an instrument as with its construction. A cabinetmaker once told me that the secret of a good finishing job is in the sanding.

The body of the instrument now should be in pretty good shape. Unless you have scratched the plywood, all it needs is the final sanding. Use caution in working with wood—especially plywood. Care must be taken that deep scratches are not made in the wood after the initial stages. Scratches must be sanded out. The veneer on the plywood is thin and it will not take too much sanding. Scrape away all the glue spots that are on the wood surface before final sanding.

The condition of the neck will determine whether you will need to use coarse paper on the neck. When all the scratches have been sanded off the neck, use a finishing sandpaper and sand the entire instrument. Each minute scratch in the wood will show through the finish.

The next step in finishing an instrument is the staining. Use good judgement in the selection of stain. An instrument first can be given a coat of light stain. Then the sides and back can be given a second coat of the same shade of stain. A light and dark colored stain can be used on the same instrument. The top can be stained a lighter shade than the rest of the body. If I make a top out of mahogany, then I will perhaps use a brown mahogany stain on the rest of the body. You can always seek advice about matching stains where supplies are purchased. Take scraps of the wood to the store (especially if one part of the instrument will not be stained). By doing this, you can usually get a good match.

Almost any of the better-quality finishing materials on the market today can be used. Most products do as much or more than the manufacturer guarantees.

There are oil finishes recommended especially for musical instruments. Also, oil for gun stocks can be used and it will provide a good finish.

If you are inexperienced in finishing wood, you could show your instrument to someone who makes his livelihood working with wood (perhaps a cabinetmaker or a person who rebuilds furniture). Ask him about staining and the finishing coats. Your time will be well spent.

Consider using a paste wax after the instrument has been finished.

# Suppliers

Listed below are addresses of suppliers of luthier materials.

**Vitali Import Co.**
5944-48 Atlantic Boulevard
Maywood, CA 90270

**Stewart-MacDonald Mfg. Co.**
Box 900
Athens, OH 45701

**J. F. Wallo Enterprises**          *S.A.S.E. requested when*
1300 G. Street N.W. (4th Floor)          *writing for catalog*
Washington, DC 20005

# Index